Family Friendly
HIKES IN MAINE

Aislinn Sarnacki

Down East Books

Dedicated to my big Maine family

Published by Down East Books
An imprint of Globe Pequot

Distributed by NATIONAL BOOK NETWORK

Copyright © 2017 by Aislinn Sarnacki

Maps: Melissa Baker © 2017 Rowman & Littlefield
All images by the author unless otherwise credited

British Library Cataloguing in Publication Information Available

Library of Congress Cataloging-in-Publication Data

Names: Sarnacki, Aislinn, 1988- author.
Title: Family-friendly hikes in Maine / Aislinn Sarnacki.
Description: Camden, Maine ; Guilford, Connecticut : Down East Books, 2017. |
    Includes index.
Identifiers: LCCN 2017005452 (print) | LCCN 2017010985 (ebook) | ISBN
    9781608935857 (pbk. : alk. paper) | ISBN 9781608935864 (e-book) | ISBN
    9781608935864 (ebook)
Subjects: LCSH: Hiking—Maine—Guidebooks. | Trails—Maine—Guidebooks. |
    Maine—Guidebooks.
Classification: LCC GV199.42.M2 S27 2017 (print) | LCC GV199.42.M2 (ebook) |
    DDC 796.5109741—dc23
LC record available at https://lccn.loc.gov/2017005452

∞™ The paper used in this publication meets the minimum requirements of American National Standard for Information Sciences—Permanence of Paper for Printed Library Materials, ANSI/NISO Z39.48-1992.

Printed in the United States of America

Contents

Acknowledgments

While I often hike solo, I'm never alone. It's extremely difficult to count the number of family, friends, colleagues, and even complete strangers who have helped me—directly or indirectly—produce this book.

That being said, I'd like to acknowledge the *Bangor Daily News* and Down East Books in particular for working with me to make this guidebook a reality. Thank you, Michael Steere from Down East Books for giving me a shot, Anthony Ronzio and Sarah Walker Caron from *Bangor Daily News* for supporting the collaboration, and Caroline McManus from Globe Pequot for giving the whole thing a close eye and making edits that truly made a difference.

I'd also like to thank my mother, Joyce Clark Sarnacki, who helped edit drafts and offered advice when I needed it most. And I'd like to thank my two most devoted hiking buddies, my husband Derek and our dog Oreo, for their limitless patience, love and support on and off the trails.

Last but not least, I'd like to thank all the people who have read my BDN column and blog over the years. Without your support, my writing wouldn't have snowballed into a book.

Introduction

With grass stains on her knees and pine needles in her tangled hair, a young girl wades through tall ferns into a woodland clearing. She pauses to tilt her face to the sky, and the summer sun makes her freckles pop. As rooted as the trees surrounding her, she stands still and enjoys the warmth of the summer and the familiar scent of balsam fir.

Perhaps she's listening to the sweet song of the hermit thrush, or maybe she's lost in thought, hatching a plan for the day's adventures. Later that day, she'll convince her big sister to join her in picking wild raspberries across the road, and then they'll ride their bikes half a mile to the ice cream stand.

Clouds sneak over the sun, and the girl opens her eyes. She takes a deep breath of fresh air, then continues on her way, through the shaded forest she knows so well.

That was about 20 years ago, and that young girl was me.

The forest behind my family home was my playground. The peaceful fern clearing was just one of the many places I remember visiting time and time again as I roamed through the golden and paper birch, sugar maples, and tall white pines. In that forest I once encountered a white-tailed deer. We were both startled to see each other as we crested the hill of hardwoods. I stood in awe as it bounded away, its fluffy white tail dancing.

Closer to home, in a shaded corner of our yard, a soft bed of moss grew. I liked to cross over it in bare feet as I walked to the nearby spring. There on a boulder I'd sit and listen to the water gurgling underground. It brought me comfort and helped me think clearly about my small problems.

I was lucky. Growing up in the 1990s, I learned to love the outdoors at an early age from my parents. My father, a lifelong hunter, angler, and gardener, taught me to ride a bike, shoot a bow, fish for pickerel and trout, canoe quiet streams, and plant vegetables. My mother shared my love for hiking, and my aunts and uncles also enjoyed camping and trekking up mountains.

In the winter my father often joined my sister and me outdoors to build snowmen and ice forts, ice-skate and ice-fish, and sled down some questionable hills. My sister and I were not forced to spend time outdoors; we chose to because it was fun. Often, we would play outside until it grew dark, our eyes adjusting to the gloom, and our parents would have to call us indoors for supper.

My family owned about 5 acres near the end of a dead-end road. We had a large yard bordered by a mixed forest. My father tended a small number of young apple trees, and each year, he planted a vegetable garden with several rows of corn, peas, carrots, cucumbers, potatoes, and beets. We always grew a clump of dill, which we used to season salmon, and hills of summer squash, winter squash, and pumpkins that we'd carve into jack-o'-lanterns in the fall. My father also grew several types of tomatoes, which he stewed into the best spaghetti sauce in the world.

Someday, I want to create something like that childhood for my own children—days filled with adventures, creativity, and healthy outdoor activity.

Someday, I imagine my children will look at me with awe when I tell them that when I was a little girl, we didn't have cell phones, and for a long time, we didn't have a computer and our television only played five local channels.

Throughout my childhood, technology rapidly improved. Music transitioned from cassette tapes and boom boxes, to CDs and Discmans, to MP3s and iPods.

Like most families in Maine, we were slightly behind on the trends. Cable television wasn't available on our rural road, but we eventually purchased a giant satellite dish, which tuned us into the vast and addictive world of channel surfing.

My family purchased our first home computer, a Windows 95, before I hit 10 years of age, and I quickly became the most knowledgeable person in the family about the machine. Sitting in front of its screen, I played pinball, raced cars, and downloaded songs using painfully slow dial-up Internet. At the time, the World Wide Web was a new and wondrous place.

In the year 2000—after the madness that was "Y2K"—I was on the verge of my teenage years and spending more time on the computer than ever before.

Also during that time, I discovered video games on Nintendo, SEGA, Playstation, and XBox. My friends and I would have slumber parties during which we'd sit in front of the TV for hours, playing video games—much like kids do today. Our video games were just a little grainier and simpler, but to us, they were remarkably high-tech and just as addictive.

Of all the technology I embraced during that time, the camcorder was probably the only thing that kept me active and constantly creating. Unfortunately, the battery power of our family camcorder was so weak that we were limited to using it indoors, where we could plug it into a wall outlet. Propping that clunky machine on a shoulder or table, my friends and I would film our own sitcoms and bogus commercials, dance routines and puppet shows.

In my teenage years, I discovered e-mail and AOL instant messenger. And upon entering high school, I received my first cell phone, a bulky Nokia that today is referred to as the infamous "brick phone." It didn't have a camera or Internet capabilities, but it did have text messaging. And it didn't take long for mobile phones to advance. By the end of high school, I was toting around a smartphone, and upon departure for college, I received my first laptop.

I think it is a combination of this new technology and the culture of high school that caused me to drift away from spending time outdoors. Thanks to school sports teams, I remained active, but I was no longer engaging with nature as I did on a daily basis as a child. I no longer simply walked in the woods.

It wasn't until college, when I moved to the great city of Boston, that I realized how important the wilderness was to me. Homesick, I would often wander into a city garden and sit among the flowers and bushes in a spot where I couldn't see the surrounding skyscrapers.

I ended up transferring to the University of Maine in Orono, and while there I reconnected with the outdoors, mostly through hiking. Spending time outdoors became necessary for me to maintain good health—physically, mentally, and emotionally. Nowadays, I cannot go without it.

The bottom line: Nature is good for you. You can sift through as many self-help books as you'd like to gain insight into why that is. Recently, multiple studies have been conducted across the globe to uncover the benefits of fresh air and outdoor exploration. But for me, experiencing it is enough. Now that I spend more time outside, I can actually feel the stress build when circumstances keep me indoors too long.

Some outdoor writers have suggested that it has a lot to do with our senses. Indoors, in front of the television or on the computer, we're often using only a couple. Mainly sight. And even then, after a while our eyes start to sting due to the unnatural light of a computer or TV screen.

Outdoors, on the other hand, you are constantly bombarded with scents and sounds, sights and feelings. The trees sway and rustle. The forest smells rich and earthy. The birds sing and fly overhead. The grass is cool and soft. In the wilderness you often use all of your senses, which makes it easier to be present and means you aren't dwelling on the past or worrying about the future—things we as humans spend a lot of energy doing.

Today, finding time to be active outdoors is easy for me because it's a part of my job.

Since 2010 I've been a full-time writer for the Outdoors section of the *Bangor Daily News*, covering topics such as outdoor recreation, conservation, and wildlife. And for five of those years, I've been in charge of a weekly column on hiking, for which I visit different trails in Maine. Over the years, I've visited at least 250 different trails throughout the state.

People often ask me, "Are you running out of places to hike yet?" And my answer is a resounding "no." Trails are all over the place in this state, and no two trails are the same.

For me, returning to the outdoors was fairly easy because I had all of those childhood experiences to fall back on. I feel comfortable in the woods—at home, even. But many people don't have those childhood experiences, so they often feel uncomfortable in the wilderness. It's more of a struggle for them to form a relationship with nature.

That makes me worried for today's youth. The technology that pulled me indoors for my teen years is nothing compared to what children are armed with today. Today, babies play apps on mobile phones. Toddlers have favorite websites, and kids are creating their own online worlds on tablets. Technology offers entertainment, usually without requiring any physical effort. It's easy. It's comfortable. It's addictive. And it's not real.

I understand the lure of it. I myself am a regular user of social media, and on occasion I get wrapped up in some online game. I'm not wagging my finger at today's children and telling them that they're doing something wrong. I'm wagging my finger at today's children and telling them that there's something that many of them are missing.

Fresh air. The beauty of nature. The joy of physical exertion.

I believe that people need to carve time out of their daily lives for the outdoors, that people should rest their eyes by walking away from the computer screen. And I believe that doing this can improve people's health tenfold. Even if there weren't research to back me up, I'd believe this from experience. Once you get in the habit of spending time outdoors each week, you feel terrible if you go without it.

I worry that many of today's children, with technology at their fingertips, won't learn the value of spending time outdoors unless they're taught by their parents—or grandparents, or some other guardian or mentor. And if they don't spend time outdoors early in life, I believe it will be much harder for them to embrace an outdoor lifestyle later, even if they want to. Without childhood memories of the wilderness, without that early familiarity with trees and wild animals and insects and dirt, the wilderness can seem a scary, unpredictable, messy place.

That's why I wanted to write this guidebook. I want to help people of all ages get to know the wilderness in Maine. I want to make it easy for people to get outside and learn about nature in beautiful, safe settings.

I understand that not everyone has 5 acres of wilderness to call their own, as I did as a child, so I'm going to tell you about some public spots you can explore. And believe me, there are so many public trails and parks in this big state, I'm only going to be able to give you the tip of the iceberg in the following pages.

The trails in this book are in the "easy" category, but keep in mind that the trails vary greatly within that grouping. Some of the trails are smooth and wide enough for wheelchairs and strollers to travel, while others are narrow and run over uneven terrain. I have done my best to describe these trails in great detail so you can decide which are best for you and your family.

My goal is to offer trails from all over the state that people of all ages can explore together. I've selected trails that I've found especially interesting for a variety of reasons. Some include built-in scavenger hunts and other outdoor games, while other trails are enhanced with colorful educational displays about nature and history. My hope is that you, the reader, will visit one or more of these trails, and by doing that, get to know the wilderness a bit better.

One word of encouragement I can give is this: In all the years I have spent seeking out Maine trails and documenting them, there has never been a time when I've finished a hike and said, "I wish I hadn't hiked today" or "It wasn't worth the drive." Not once.

Hiking Through Life

At the age of five, my niece Willamina has now mastered the art of walking over narrow bog bridges. She has also learned how to identify cinnamon ferns and bunchberries, and she has overcome her fear of dragonflies. She is a most eye-opening hiking companion, showing great wonder for beautiful scenes in nature that I often take for granted.

I hope that her early discoveries in nature will encourage her to care about the environment and to continue to enjoy the benefits of outdoor activities her whole life long. I hope to show her one way to do that is through hiking.

Hiking—the way I choose to define it—is a lifelong sport.

My personal definition of hiking is "walking in a wilderness area of any kind." A hike doesn't have to include a mountain or any other specific natural feature. A hike can be on an easy path or a challenging mountain trail. Hiking can take days, or it can take 20 minutes. My definition of the activity is very broad.

Using that definition of hiking, I'd like to think that hiking is for everyone, even people who use wheelchairs or another device to assist their mobility. Hiking is for babies and elderly people and everyone in between—given the right trail.

This book of "family friendly" hikes will feature easy trails, some of which were constructed to be wheelchair accessible by ADA standards. While some families can certainly tackle very strenuous hikes, I chose easy hikes because I think these are accessible to more families—families with young children, for instance, and families that includes grandparents and great-grandparents.

My belief that hiking can be a lifelong sport has been strengthened by meeting hikers of all ages through my career as a newspaper reporter whose beat includes outdoor activities. A few names come to mind in particular.

Neva Warren, 15, of Florida, hiked 2,200 miles along the Appalachian Mountain Range from Georgia to Maine in 2013 to become the youngest solo thru-hiker to complete the famous Appalachian Trail. I met up with this inspiring young woman in Monson, Maine, just about a week before she completed her long trek. We sat at a picnic table and talked about long-distance hiking, and the importance of fingernail polish and good music while on the trail.

Hiking is different for everyone.

Then there's David Thompson, a retired forester who at 78 was maintaining hiking trails in Orono as one of the most active volunteers of the Orono Land Trust. On a sunny day in July of 2015, I went on a walk with him in one of the preserves he helps manage. He pointed out invasive plants and explained the different life spans of the different materials used to create footbridges. He was healthy and energetic and generous with his time. I strive to age (or refuse to age) in a similar fashion.

He's not the only older person I've met on the trail. In fact, most people I meet on the trail are older than I am. But it doesn't matter. In the wilderness, for me, people's differences—including age differences—seem to melt away because we know that we all have one important thing in common: we're all actively enjoying nature.

And we're all benefiting from it. Trust me.

The Scariest Creature in the Maine Woods

More than once people planning to visit Maine have e-mailed me to ask about local wildlife. Specifically, they want to know about any animals that might be dangerous if they spend time outside hiking or camping. I always give them the same answer: Beware of ticks.

Black bears, moose, coyotes, bobcats, and Canada lynx—all powerful mammals found in Maine—rarely cause people any trouble. In fact, if you see any of these wild animals, they'll likely run the other way. Maine doesn't have any poisonous snakes and our water critters are pretty low key.

But ticks—tiny pests that belong to the arachnid family and feed on blood—are another story. They're truly the most dangerous creature in the Maine woods today. Different species of ticks are capable of carrying different diseases, which they can transfer to people and pets through their bite.

When I was a little girl, ticks weren't a problem. We simply didn't have them in Maine. But over the past decade or so, ticks have migrated north and into our beautiful state. Now, at least 14 different species of ticks have made their home here, according to the University of Maine Tick Identification Lab.

Of those species, the most worrisome is the blacklegged tick, also known as the deer tick, which is the only species capable of transmitting Lyme disease, an illness that usually starts out with flu-like symptoms and attacks various body systems. If left untreated, Lyme disease can be life threatening. Fortunately doctors can detect and treat the disease with antibiotics. But if a person isn't diagnosed and treated early, the disease may become chronic.

The first documented case of Lyme disease in Maine was in 1986. Since then the blacklegged tick has spread throughout the state, infiltrating every single county and causing more than 1,000 new cases of Lyme disease annually.

I don't want to scare you out of the Maine woods. Ticks and the diseases they carry are spread throughout the United States; Connecticut, Massachusetts, New Jersey, New York, and especially Pennsylvania, consistently report more new cases of Lyme disease annually than Maine. Yet people are still enjoying the outdoors. They just need to take more precautions.

Ticks can be actively seeking a host any time the temperature rises above 38 degrees Fahrenheit, according to the University of Maine Tick Identification Lab. In Maine, the blacklegged tick is most active in the spring and fall, with a lull in activity during the summer, when it's typically too dry for them, and during the winter, when they hibernate.

When a tick is looking for "blood meal," it often perches on the end of a blade of grass or foliage, then reaches out with its long front legs and grabs at whatever brushes by. The tick crawls around on its host and finds a spot on the skin to bite. It then burrow its mouthparts into the skin and start sucking, filling its round body up with blood. The tick may feed for days or weeks, depending on the species of tick and its stage of life.

Is your skin crawling yet? I'm guessing you want to know how to protect yourself against these nasty little creatures.

The most important thing you can do is to check yourself for ticks after spending time outdoors. If you're travelling in a vehicle, do a tick check before you get into the car. At home, shake out your clothes and put them in the washing machine. Then, because ticks are hard to drown, you'll want to put those clothes in the dryer, on high heat. But most importantly, check your whole body with your eyes and hands. Be sure to check all the nooks and crannies, where ticks love to hide. And remember that a young tick is about the size of a freckle.

Tick checks are easier to do with a partner you feel comfortable with. I once asked the assistance of my niece who was 3 years old at the time, and she teased me by pretending she found "a bug" on my back. She then let me check her for ticks. I resisted the impulse to tease her back.

It may seem overkill, but you should check your body for ticks more than once after coming indoors. I'll never forget the time I was looking in the bathroom mirror and watched a tick crawl out of my hair and across my forehead. Ticks are good at hiding, and they're so small that they're easily overlooked.

Fortunately, there are some things you can do to discourage ticks from crawling on you in the first place. Here are a few:

- Expose less skin. Wear pants instead of shorts, and while it may not be fashionable, tuck the bottom of your pants into your socks. This greatly reduces your chances of a tick scurrying up your leg.
- Wear light-colored clothing so you can more easily see ticks and brush them off before they find your skin.
- Treat your clothing with a chemical called permethrin, which has proven effective in deterring ticks. Do not spray this on your skin.
- Use an all-natural tick repellent, such as Green Mountain Tick Repellent made in Vermont.
- Avoiding wading through grass or underbrush, which is prime tick habitat.

If you do find a tick on you, your first impulse will probably be to tear it out of your skin—but don't. It's important to remove the tick in a certain way in order to reduce your chances of contracting any illness it's carrying. There are old wives' tales about using a hot match or nail polish remover to deal with a tick. Please don't do either of those things. These methods may cause the tick to regurgitate into your bloodstream, which could transmit disease.

What you should do is take a pair of tweezers (or a nifty little device called a tick spoon) and grasp the tick firmly as close to your skin as possible. Then slowly pull the tick away from you with steady pressure until it releases. The goal is to get the entire tick out of your skin, but if you leave some mouthparts behind, it's been found that it won't cause any further problems. Your skin will eventually push the mouthparts out.

After that's done, don't smash the tick to kill it. Its body could explode, and if the innards of a tick somehow get into a wound on your skin, it could transmit a disease. Simply flush the tick down the toilet or put it in a baggy if you want it to be tested for disease at the nearest tick-borne disease lab. It's also a good idea to contact a doctor to talk about whether you should take antibiotics to nip any potential tick-borne disease in the bud.

Bottom line—be aware, be informed, and be vigilant, but don't be afraid. Spending time outdoors is way too much fun to give up.

Preparing for Your Hike

With any outdoor adventure, no matter how small, preparation is key to having a safe, enjoyable time. It doesn't have to be complicated or time-consuming. But trust me, putting in just a little bit of effort before your adventure can really make a difference in the amount of fun you have while on the trail.

The first thing I do when planning a hike is pick a trail and learn about it. These are some of the questions I try to find the answers to: What are the trail rules? Are dogs allowed, and if they are, do they need to be on a leash of specific length? What's the trail like? Where can I get a map? In what form do I want to carry that map? How long will the drive take to get to the trailhead? Is the trail even accessible this time of year? (In Maine, a lot of roads that lead to the remoter trails aren't plowed during the winter.)

This guide makes it possible for you to answer those questions without looking anywhere else.

It's also helpful to learn about who owns and manages the trail. Trails are owned and maintained by towns, land trusts, the state and federal governments, schools, and other entities. Often, these trail owners have websites or offices where you can gather additional information. For example, in this guidebook, I have included a preserve that is owned and maintained by the Blue Hill Heritage Trust. This particular land trust conserves land and maintains more than 20 public hiking trails throughout the Blue Hill Peninsula, and all of them are listed on the land trust website, bluehillheritagetrust.org.

So, while I've selected 35 of my favorite family friendly hikes to describe in detail in this guidebook, the information I provide about trail maintainers and owners in this book will serve as a gateway for you to learn about many more trails throughout Maine.

Next in the preparation process: You'll need a backpack—not a tote or a purse—a backpack. I don't care how short or easy the trail is, it's always good to carry a few items with you, and I believe a backpack is the best way to carry them. Because a backpack is carried on your back, it's out of the way and leaves your hands free to maintain balance, hold someone's hand, take photos or unfold a trail map. Specifically, I prefer a backpack that secures with simple straps and buckles around my waist and across my chest so it doesn't shift every time I bend over to look at a wildflower.

So now that I hope you're convinced that a backpack is necessary, here's a few items you may want to consider putting into the backpack:

- Water—more than you think you'll need.
- Tasty snacks. In the summer, choose snacks that won't squish or spoil in the heat. And if it's winter, select snacks that won't freeze.
- Small first aid kit
- Headlamp or flashlight (with extra batteries)
- Compass and trail map

- Cell phone (charged)
- Rain jacket
- Extra layers of clothing, depending on the weather
- Camera (so you can take photos and leave nature as you find it)

During the winter or during longer hikes, I'd also consider packing:

- Handwarmers
- Extra mittens
- Fire starter
- Space blanket
- GPS device
- Satellite tracking device, such as SPOT Satellite Messenger

These are just a few suggestions. I've heard it said that a day hiker should carry enough supplies to get them through a night in the woods . . . just in case. But no one said that night has to be comfortable, so you don't have to go overboard. The likelihood of you getting stuck in the woods overnight is slim, but it's not unheard of.

For even more ideas about what to pack while day hiking, one of the best sources I've found is the Appalachian Mountain Club website, outdoors.org.

So now it's time for me to confess. I'm not the best at preparing or packing for adventures, but I'm a lot better than I used to be.

For the most part, I have learned the hard way. For instance, I didn't think a first aid kit was necessary on a day hike until I fell on exposed bedrock on Old Speck Mountain in western Maine. I was OK, but both of my knees and hands were torn up and bleeding. I wasn't far from my car, so I just kept going. Eventually I hiked by a group of Boy Scouts heading in the opposite direction. The boys looked at me with horror and asked if I was OK and if I needed some bandages. Well, yes, I did, but I stubbornly declined their kind offer and continued down the mountain. How embarrassing.

I could go on and on, telling you about the time I didn't have an updated trail map or the time I lost a mitten on the trail, but I think you get the idea. Pack items that will help you stay safe, happy, and comfortable on the trail. You won't regret it.

And last but perhaps most importantly, tell someone about your plans. Actually, write out your plans or send an explicit text. Tell them where you're going and when you plan to return. This is your safety net, so make sure this person is responsible and attentive. If you don't return when you say you will, that person will know exactly where to start looking . . . because let's face it, accidents happen. Maybe you twisted your ankle or took the wrong turn. You can't predict these things. However, I will point out that accidents are a lot less likely to happen if you plan your adventure, and accidents are a lot easier to handle if you've packed emergency supplies and have someone at home who knows where you are and is waiting for your return.

Now get outside and hike already!

Map Legend

=⟨201⟩=	US Highway		Boat Launch
=⟨17⟩=	State Road		Bridge
	Local/County Road	▪	Building/Point of Interest
====:	Unpaved Road	▲	Campground
⊢—•—⊣	Railroad	⏐	Gate
------	Trail		Lighthouse
	Body of Water	🅿	Parking
	Marsh	▲	Peak/Elevation
	Beach	🇦	Picnic Area
	Park/Wilderness/Preserve		Ranger Station/Park Office
	River		Restroom
	Intermittent Stream		Scenic View
	Waterfall		Trailhead
⌀	Spring	❓	Visitor/Information Center
	Bench		Water
‖‖‖‖	Boardwalk/Steps	♿	Wheelchair Accessible

Hike 1: Hidden Valley Nature Center in Jefferson

About these trails: Founded as a wildlife refuge and public recreation area in 2009 by David "Tracy" Moskovitz and his wife, Bambi Jones, Hidden Valley Nature Center covers about 1,000 acres of diverse habitats in the central Maine town of Jefferson. With a growing group of devoted volunteers, the couple developed a 25-mile trail system on the property, as well as a bog boardwalk, campsites, a group shelter, a nature center, and a yurt and cabins for overnight visitors to rent.

Difficulty: Easy to strenuous, depending on the trails you choose and the time of year. Trail difficulty is labeled on the map displayed on a kiosk near the parking area. The trails closest to the main parking area are easy, smooth forest paths that feature a trail game for children and a bog boardwalk. The trails farther from the parking area are more challenging, as they travel over steep hills and along a rocky bluff.

Dogs: Permitted off leash if well behaved and responsive to voice command. Otherwise, dogs are permitted on leash. Visitors are expected to pick up after their dogs and dispose of waste properly.

Cost: The center asks for a $5 day-use donation to be left at the kiosk near the parking area.

Access: No motorized vehicles. Trails are for hiking, mountain biking, horseback riding, snowshoeing, and skiing. Rental canoes are available at the center for use on Little Dyer Pond, and there are six options for people who wish to stay overnight on the property.

Wheelchair accessibility: Trails are not built to ADA standards, though the Midcoast Conservancy is considering future projects to develop some trails on the property with those standards. Many of the trails and woods roads on the property have the potential to be traveled by wheelchair, depending on the wheelchair and the ability of the person operating it.

Hunting: Not permitted.

Restrooms: For day-use visitors, two outhouses are located by the big barn on the property. For those renting cabins, campsites, or the yurt, all have their own outhouses.

How to get there: The address is 131 Egypt Road in Jefferson. Starting at the intersection of Route 194 (Jones Woods Road) and Route 215 (S Clary Road) in Newcastle, drive on Route 215 for 4.4 miles and turn left onto Egypt Road. Drive 0.5 mile and the gate parking area will be on your right, just before the gate, which bars visitors from the center's service road. Hike up the service road and you will come to a kiosk on the right, which includes a donation box, trail maps, and plenty of information about the center.

GPS coordinates: 44.146023', -69.569256'

In January 2016 the nonprofit Hidden Valley Nature Center merged with the Midcoast Conservancy, which now leases the property and maintains the trails and facilities. The conservancy also runs recreation programs and nature programs at HVNC year-round.

Spring through fall, the trails on the property are used by hikers, horseback riders, and mountain bikers; and in the winter HVNC turns into a playground for cross-country skiers and snowshoers, with groomed trails and warming huts.

The Kettle Hole Bog Boardwalk travels out into a small peat bog and features interpretive displays about the bog's fascinating flora, including three carnivorous plants: roundleaf sundews, pitcher plants and bladderwort.

One way HVNC keeps younger visitors active and engaged is by offering two trail games.

On the Warbler's Way trail, which begins right at the main parking area, is a one-of-a-kind scavenger hunt developed by local game designer Aaron Weissblum. The game includes colorful wooden figures called "Trail Guys," which have been posted on trees along the trail. The goal of the game is to find each Trail Guy—which wear symbols and corresponding letters on their chests—and use them to decode a message on the game sheet, which is available at the kiosk by the main parking area. Once solved, the message will direct you to a "scroll," on which you can write your name and e-mail to be entered into a drawing for various prizes.

The second game, "The Woods of HVNC Quest," was recently created by HVNC interns Kelley Kasper and Sarah Weinberg. This quest is a natural history tour of the working woods and leads visitors along a mile-long route starting near the main parking area.

Details about both of these games are available at the Gate House, which is a kiosk just a short walk from the main parking lot on an easy, wide trail. Details about the games are also available at Hi-Hut, a visitor center located near "The Barn" group shelter in a central clearing in the trail network. This is also where most public programs take place.

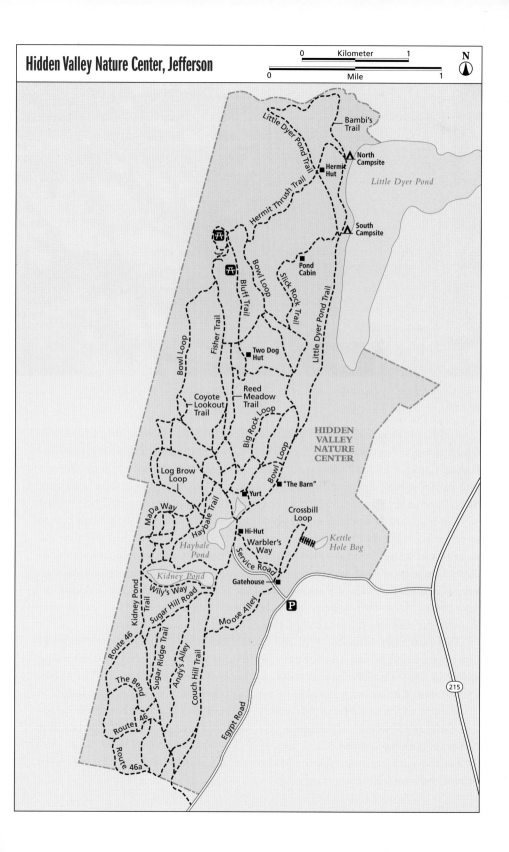

Hidden Valley Nature Center, Jefferson

Kilometer
0 ... 1

Mile
0 ... 1

N

Bambi's Trail

Little Dyer Pond Trail

North Campsite

Hermit Hut

Little Dyer Pond

Hermit Thrush Trail

South Campsite

Pond Cabin

Bowl Loop

Bluff Trail

Slick Rock Trail

Fisher Trail

Bowl Loop

Little Dyer Pond Trail

Two Dog Hut

Reed Meadow Trail

Coyote Lookout Trail

Big Rock Loop

Bowl Loop

HIDDEN VALLEY NATURE CENTER

Log Brow Loop

Yurt

"The Barn"

MaDa Way

Crossbill Loop

Haybale Trail

Hi-Hut

Warbler's Way

Kettle Hole Bog

Haybale Pond

Service Road

Kidney Pond

Gatehouse

Wily's Way

Route 46 Kidney Pond Trail

Sugar Hill Road

P

Sugar Ridge Trail

Moose Alley

Andy's Alley

Couch Hill Trail

The Bend

Route 46

Egypt Road

215

Route 46a

Identification tags like this help visitors learn about a variety of trees throughout the trail network.

Another highlight of HVNC's trail network is the Kettle Hole Bog Boardwalk, which is just a short walk from the parking lot on the Warbler's Way trail and connecting Crossbill Loop. Traveling out into a small peat bog, the wide boardwalk leads to a platform with interpretive displays about the bog's fascinating flora, including three carnivorous plants: roundleaf sundews, pitcher plants, and horned bladderwort.

The trails farther from the main parking area become increasingly difficult as they travel over a ridge on the property to partial views of the region, then down to the shore of Little Dyer Pond, where you may spy an osprey, Canada geese, or a variety of ducks. These more challenging trails visit a number of natural features including vernal pools, glacial erratics, and small ponds that are abundant in wildlife. Educational signs posted along the way help visitors learn more about these features and identify many of the different trees on the property.

Two easy trails—Bambi's Trail and Little Dyer Pond Trail—trace the shore of Little Dyer Pond, which is a nice place for a quiet paddle, a swim, or some fishing. There are canoes available to rent at the pond, as well as two campsites and Little Dyer Pond Cabin, with all three available for rent for people looking to stay overnight.

In addition, there are two rustic cabins—Hermit Hut and Two Dog Hut—available for rent elsewhere on the property, as well as a spacious yurt. Altogether, that makes six camping options.

For more information: Call the Midcoast Conservancy office at (207) 389-5150 or visit www.midcoastconservancy.org.

Personal note: Hidden Valley Nature Center first caught my attention when I was putting together the events calendar for the *Bangor Daily News* Outdoors section—a tedious task, but one that keeps me up to date about what organizations in Maine are offering outdoorsy events for the public. HVNC kept popping up, offering everything from chainsaw safety courses to mushroom walks to biathlons for beginners. As it turns out, the center hosts about 50 public programs each year.

I'd never been to Jefferson, so naturally, I Googled it, and on Google maps, HVNC looked pretty gigantic in comparison to some of the other outdoor locales I've visited. I couldn't believe I'd never heard any of my friends or family talk about it. It was only an hour and a half from my Bangor-area home, which, if you live in Maine, isn't a very long drive. In Maine, where there are about 17.8 million acres of forestland covering nearly 90 percent of the state and only 1.3 million people (that's one person per 13.6 acres of forest, roughly), things are fairly spread out. That's just the way it is.

Colorful wooden figures called "Trail Guys" can be found throughout the trail network and are a part of a special trail game designed for the property.

It was a sunny, windless August day when I arrived at HVNC with my dog, Oreo, to explore the trail network. First, I needed to slather my body in bug repellent to fend off hordes of mosquitoes and deer flies. Thus prepared, I headed up the wide trail and soon spotted the Gate House—a sheltered kiosk plastered with information about the center, including a detailed trail map.

Soon into my visit, I came across David "Tracy" Moskovitz and his wife, Bambi Jones, the founders of HVNC, and they paused in their work to tell me about the ongoing projects and events at the center.

After bidding them goodbye, I headed out on the trail system, wandering it with a trail map in my hand lest I get hopelessly lost in the 1,000 acres of woodland, hills, and ponds.

On the bog boardwalk, I kept Oreo on a short leash so he wouldn't dive into the deep sphagnum moss and destroy delicate plants in his attempt to explore. But as we walked along the shore of Little Dyer Pond, Oreo waded into the water, disturbing the smooth surface, which perfectly reflected the blue sky, white puffy clouds, and a jagged row of evergreens growing along the shore.

Some trails were wide, others were narrow, a few were overgrown, but for the most part, the trails were well maintained and marked with signs. Nevertheless, I advise you carry a trail map during your first, second, and even third visit. The trail network is vast and can be confusing. And don't count on seeing everything in one day. I walked for hours and only made it to about half of the places I wanted to visit.

Hike 2: Wolfe's Neck Woods State Park in Freeport

About these trails: Just minutes from downtown Freeport, Wolfe's Neck Woods State Park was gifted to the state by Mr. and Mrs. Lawrence M. C. Smith of Freeport in 1969. Approximately 200 acres in size, the park features about 4.5 miles of well-groomed trails that lead visitors to a variety of habitats, including white pine and hemlock forests, a salt marsh estuary, mixed hardwood stands, the rocky coast on Casco Bay, and the mouth of the Harraseeket River.

Difficulty: Easy to moderate. The extensive trail network—about 4.5 miles of intersecting walking paths—travels over relatively even terrain.

Dogs: Permitted but must be on leash at all times. Visitors are expected to pick up after their dogs and dispose of waste properly.

Cost: $4 for adult Maine residents, $6 for adult nonresidents, $2 for senior nonresidents, $1 for children 5–11 years old, free for children under 5 years old, and free for Maine seniors (65+).

Access: Open 9 a.m. to sunset daily, year-round, unless otherwise signed at the gate. Camping and fires are not permitted. Trails are for foot traffic only. Bikes are not allowed.

Wheelchair accessibility: A good portion of the trail network is wheelchair accessible. In the trail brochure and displayed on the trailhead kiosk are six hiking route suggestions, and two of those are wheelchair accessible: the Osprey Tour, which is 0.2 mile one way, and the Forest and Shore Tour, a 0.75-mile loop. Also, some of the restrooms are built to be wheelchair accessible.

Hunting: Not permitted.

Restrooms: Restrooms are located at the main parking area by the field.

How to get there: From Route 1 in the bustling town of Freeport, turn onto Bow Street, which is across the road from the L.L. Bean flagship store. Drive about 2.4 miles, then turn right onto Wolfe's Neck Road. Drive about 1.5 miles and the park entrance will be on the left. Pay the park admission fee at the entrance gate before parking in one of the two large parking areas.

GPS coordinates: 43.825823', -70.085570'

Most park visitors start their outing at one of the kiosks by the parking areas, where trail maps are on display and suggested hiking routes are described.

Of the many trails, the 0.5-mile Casco Bay Trail may be the most popular. This loop trail starts at the field by the main parking area and leads to the coast, to views of Eagle, Googins, and Cousin Islands. Along this easy hike, side trails provide access to rocky beaches, where herons are often found wading in the shallows of the bay. There's also a spot along the trail where you can observe ospreys nesting on Googins Island. This outlook includes wooden benches and an interpretive display that explains the life cycle of the bird.

For a longer, more challenging hike in the park, you can try the 1.8-mile Harraseeket Trail, which leads through the woods and across Wolfe's Neck Road, then descends gradually to run along the cliffs above the Harraseeket River. The loop hike

Googins Island Osprey Sanctuary is seen from a rocky beach of the park.

then heads back uphill, crosses back over the road, travels over two small hills, and ends at the shore, where you can take the Casco Bay Trail back to the parking lot.

Because there are so many intersecting trails that form this network, it's wise to carry a trail map with you so you don't become lost or frustrated. Other trails on the property include the Hemlock Ridge Trail, Power Line Trail, Old Woods Road Trail, North Loop Trail, and Ledge Trail, all of which have descriptive names that give you an idea of the different features on the property.

Ten interpretive displays are spaced throughout the trail network, helping visitors learn about the natural world through text, diagrams, and illustrations. The ten displays are titled "White Pines," "From Field to Forest," "Life Between the Tides," "Life in the Estuary," "Osprey Nesting Area," "The Rocky Shore," "Animals of the Bay," "Islands and Beyond," "Dry Ledges and Wet Woods," and "Of Rocks and Hemlocks."

Wolfe's Neck Woods State Park is one of the most active parks in the state park system when it comes to offering public nature programs and guided tours. And in conjunction with nearby Bradbury Mountain State Park, Wolfe's Neck hosts the annual Feathers Over Freeport birding festival each spring.

For more information: Call the park at (207) 865-4465 or visit www.maine.gov/wolfesneckwoods, where you can download a park brochure and trail map and view a calendar of upcoming events happening in the park.

Personal note: Before heading to my friend's house in Freeport for a flannel party—a fall cookout during which everyone wears their fanciest flannel shirt—my

A good portion of the trail network at the park was constructed to be wheelchair accessible.

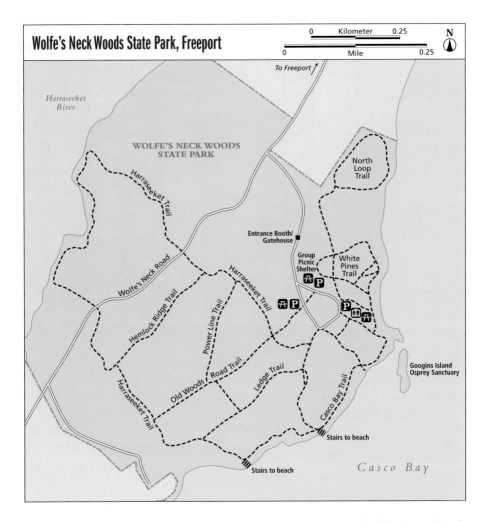

0   Kilometer   0.25

0   Mile   0.25

N

To Freeport

Harraseeket River

WOLFE'S NECK WOODS STATE PARK

North Loop Trail

Harraseeket Trail

Entrance Booth/ Gatehouse

Group Picnic Shelter

White Pines Trail

Wolfe's Neck Road

Harraseeket Trail

Hemlock Ridge Trail

Power Line Trail

Old Woods Road Trail

Ledge Trail

Casco Bay Trail

Googins Island Osprey Sanctuary

Harraseeket Trail

Stairs to beach

Stairs to beach

Casco Bay

husband, Derek, and I decided to go on a morning adventure at Wolfe's Neck Woods State Park. It was October and neither of us had been to the park before, though I'd seen fliers about the park's many family friendly programs while shopping in downtown Freeport.

We had only a few hours to spend at the park, so we planned to hurry along the trails and cover as much ground as possible. But it didn't work out that way; I got a bit distracted (which tends to happen a lot when I'm outdoors due to my love of photographing pretty much everything in nature).

First, I spotted a great blue heron wading in the ocean, so I squatted in the mud for a while to photograph the elegant bird. It was actually the first time I'd ever seen a great blue heron, though I've seen plenty since, and have even visited a great heron colony, which is basically just a group of stick nests in which they raise their young. Great blue herons are one of the largest wading birds we have in Maine, and they're

A dead horseshoe crab, a rare find, lies on the rocky beach at the park.

quite impressive to watch hunt. They have special bones in their neck that allow them to strike at their prey (typically fish and frogs) more quickly.

After the hike I did a little research on the Cornell Lab of Ornithology website—a great place to learn about birds—and found out that the heron I'd seen at Wolfe's Neck Woods State Park was a young (or juvenile) heron, since some of its adult plumage had yet to grow in.

On the beach at Wolfe's Neck, I became distracted again, and that time, it was Derek's fault. He'd found a horseshoe crab, which is quite rare in Maine. Horseshoe crabs are rather ancient sea creatures, and while they're abundant throughout the world, they spend the majority of their time feeding in the deep sea, far from land—so people don't see them that often. However, each spring, they swim ashore to spawn, typically at high tide and during the new and full moons. In Maine, the northern edge of their range, they swim ashore in only a few places.

But it was fall when we were roaming the beach of Wolfe's Neck, and the horseshoe crab, sadly, was dead. We picked it up (which required two hands because the crabs are so big) and flipped it over to see that it was indeed lifeless.

I later learned more about horseshoe crabs when I attended a horseshoe crab walk in May 2016 on the Baggaduce River, one of the places in Maine where they spawn. During the walk, which was led by the Blue Hill Heritage Trust, we observed two (live) horseshoe crabs pairing up, the male grabbing onto the female's back with his large front pincers.

Back at Wolfe's Neck Woods State Park, we left the sea behind to roam the many forest trails of the park, where we found mushrooms of all shapes and sizes. Every time we came across a new and exciting species of fungus, I'd sink to the forest floor to photograph it from a good angle. Derek may have been wishing he were sipping a nice cold beer at the flannel party at that point, but he remained patient and even pointed out a few of the mushrooms.

Needless to say, we were a bit late for the party. But when we arrived, there was a group of friends gathered around the campfire, a smorgasbord on the deck, and no need for apologies.

Hike 3: Orono Bog Boardwalk in Bangor and Orono

About this trail: Lined with cinnamon ferns, skunk cabbage, and bog maples, the Orono Bog Boardwalk begins in a forested wetland at the edge of the Rolland F. Perry City Forest, also known as the Bangor City Forest.

Difficulty: Easy. Benches are located at least every 200 feet on the boardwalk. The entire boardwalk—out, around the loop, and back—is less than 1 mile of walking. And to get to the boardwalk from the parking area, you must first walk about 0.25 mile on an easy, wide gravel trail.

Dogs: While leashed dogs are permitted on the forest trails surrounding the boardwalk, dogs are not allowed on the boardwalk for a number of reasons, including that if a dog were to step off the boardwalk, it would sink into the peat and damage fragile bog plants. If visitors bring their dogs on forest trails, they are expected to pick up after their dogs and dispose of waste properly.

Cost: Free, but donations can be made at www .umaine.edu/oronobogwalk/support.

Access: Each spring, the boardwalk opens on May 1 and remains open through late November, unless reconstruction projects change those dates.

Wheelchair accessibility: The boardwalk was constructed to be used by wheelchairs and is 4 feet wide. The trail leading to the boardwalk is wheelchair accessible as well.

Hunting: Not permitted.

Restrooms: Outhouses, including a wheelchair-accessible outhouse, are located in a clearing beside the woodland trail that leads to the boardwalk.

How to get there: From Bangor, drive toward Orono on Stillwater Avenue (by the Bangor Mall) and turn left onto Tripp Drive. Continue to the end of Tripp Drive. At the cul-de-sac, drive straight onto a dirt road, which will end in a large dirt parking lot for the Rolland F. Perry City Forest, also known as the Bangor City Forest. Park there and walk to the northeast side of the parking lot to find the wide, 0.25-mile trail that leads through the forest to the Orono Bog Boardwalk. You can refer to a detailed color map on display at the trailhead to avoid confusion.

GPS coordinates: 44.862797', -68.728449'

Constructed in 2002 and 2003 by Veazie resident Ron Davis and more than 100 volunteers, the boardwalk starts in Bangor, crosses the town line into Orono, and splits into a loop that leads visitors out into a large peat bog filled with old and stunted black spruce trees, alien-like pitcher plants, tiny pink buds of bog rosemary, white tufts of cotton sedge, and dozens of other plants that thrive only in bogs.

The boardwalk is 4,200 feet long—just under a mile—and wide enough to be accessed by wheelchairs and strollers. Along the way are benches and colorful educational displays about the flora and fauna of the bog and surrounding forest.

Jointly managed by the Orono Land Trust, the city of Bangor, and the University of Maine, the boardwalk is operated and maintained by a group of dedicated volunteers.

My niece, Willamina, touches a delicate lady's slipper growing beside a trail in the city forest.

Originally built with cedarwood, pieces of the boardwalk began decaying and breaking after about five years, and volunteers were constantly repairing it. In response, volunteers initiated the Boardwalk Campaign, a fundraising effort to replace the existing wood boardwalk with longer-lasting composite material, beginning early in 2012. Since then, sections of the boardwalk have been replaced each year.

The boardwalk is a highlight of the Rolland F. Perry City Forest, where visitors will find more than 9 miles of additional trails for walking, running, skiing, and biking. Most of the trails are easy and family friendly, and many of the small side trails are named after animals of the forest, such as the Hare Trail and Deer Trail.

For more information: Visit www.oronobogwalk.org, where you'll find maps, updates on renovations and repairs, and a calendar of free nature programs held at the boardwalk.

Personal note: The Orono Bog Boardwalk is so close to where I work and live that I usually get the chance to visit it several times each year, which is interesting because the scenery is always changing. As the weather grows warmer, ferns unfurl in the forest and pitcher plants emerge from the peat, sprouting tall stems to display their deep red and yellow flowers.

I was there May 1, 2012, when the boardwalk opened for the season and celebrated its 10th anniversary of being open to the public. It was raining that morning, and I spotted a snowshoe hare in the forest. It being so early in the year, only a few plants had started to bud.

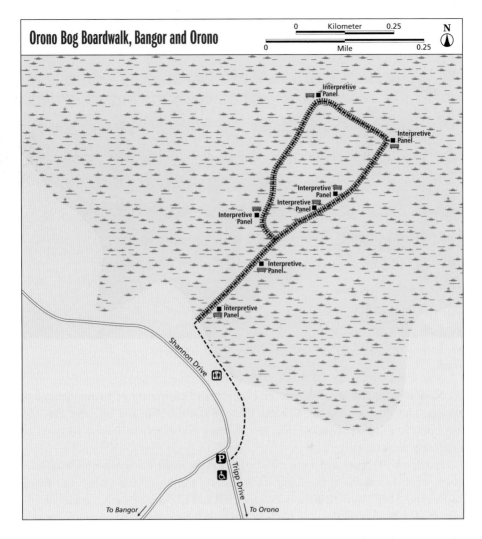

Along the boardwalk, skunk cabbage is always one of the first plants to make an appearance each year. In fact, it's known for popping up through lingering snow, emerging as a flower, then leafing out into a large, green, cabbage-like plant as the season progresses. As you may have guessed by its name, skunk cabbage doesn't smell particularly good, but it's not poisonous. In fact, the plant's foul odor actually helps attract pollinators such as bees.

I've also visited the bog twice with the founder of the boardwalk, Ron Davis, who authored the 2016 book *Bogs and Fens: A Guide to Peatland Plants of the Northeastern United States and Adjacent Canada*. I can't say enough good things about Davis, who has a great passion for birding and nature photography and gives back to the community through his volunteer work with area land trusts and, of course, the Orono Bog Boardwalk.

My niece, Willamina, walks along the Orono Bog Boardwalk, checking out all the different plants.

Now retired, Davis is professor emeritus at the University of Maine School of Biology and Ecology and the Climate Change Institute. He and his wife, Lee, live in Orono in a solar-powered home, though they find plenty of reasons to travel to exciting places together.

Perhaps my favorite experience of the boardwalk so far was in the middle of June 2016, when I introduced the Bangor City Forest and boardwalk to my dear niece, Willamina. At the time, Willa was 4½ years old and excited for such a grand adventure. On the boardwalk she took the lead, her little brown ponytail bobbing with each step, and at each interpretive display she stopped to point out illustrations of animals she recognized—a frog, a squirrel, a bird.

She'd never visited a bog before, and I didn't want to overload her with too much information, but I did point out a few different plants, including sweet pink laurel blossoms (which she insisted were actually more purple than pink) and cotton sedge, which looks like grass tipped with miniature cotton balls. She paused several times to feel the sedge's soft white tufts.

We were about halfway around the loop when I asked her, "So, what plant do you like the best?"

Walking ahead of me, Willa stopped in her tracks and stretched her arms out wide.

"All of it," she said with feeling. "I like all of it. It's brilliant."

Hike 4: Ship Harbor Nature Trail in Acadia National Park

About this trail: The Ship Harbor Nature Trail is one of several easy, family friendly hikes in Acadia National Park on scenic Mount Desert Island. Shaped like a figure eight, the trail leads to the rocky coastline and through a whimsical spruce-fir forest. Along the way beautifully illustrated nature displays help walkers interpret their surroundings.

Difficulty: Easy to moderate. The trail forms a 1.3-mile figure eight. The first loop is surfaced with gravel and very easy to travel, while the second loop is not surfaced with gravel and includes bog bridges, rocky sections, and some exposed tree roots that can easily trip people who aren't paying attention to their feet.

Dogs: Permitted if kept on a leash no longer than 6 feet at all times. Visitors are expected to pick up after their dogs and dispose of waste properly.

Cost: All park visitors are required to pay for and display a park pass upon entry May through October. The entrance pass for a passenger car is $25 and good for seven days. Annual and lifetime park passes are also available. Park passes can be purchased online at www.nps.gov/acad or at a variety of locations, including park headquarters, visitor centers, entrance stations, and campgrounds. Entrance to the park is free November through April.

Access: This trail is open year-round, though in the winter it can be dangerous due to ice. The road leading to the trailhead is open year-round, as well. Bikes, horses, camping, and fires are not permitted on or near the trail.

Wheelchair accessibility: The first loop of the figure eight trail was constructed to ADA standards to be wheelchair accessible. The second loop was not constructed to be wheelchair accessible and includes a lot of exposed tree roots and uneven terrain.

Hunting: Not permitted.

Restrooms: An outhouse is located at the trailhead, but it is open only May through October.

How to get there: Drive onto Mount Desert Island on Route 3, pass over the causeway, and veer right, heading toward Southwest Harbor on Route 102. In 5.2 miles, veer left at the fork and continue on Route 102 for 11.3 miles, passing through a light in downtown Somesville (at about 5 miles) and the town of Southwest Harbor. At 11.3 miles, you'll come to a fork; veer right onto Route 102 and drive 1.6 miles to an intersection in the town of Bass Harbor and veer left onto Route 102A. Drive 2.3 miles on that road, passing the road to Bass Harbor Head Lighthouse, and the parking lot for Ship Harbor Nature Trail will be on your right, just 0.3 mile before the Wonderland Trail park area, which also will be on your right.

GPS coordinates: 44.231720', -68.325580'

The trail starts at the parking lot and crosses a small clearing before entering the woods, where a kiosk displays a trail map and visitor guidelines. Soon after the kiosk, the trail splits into the first loop, which is wide and surfaced with gravel.

If you turn right and hike the loop counterclockwise, the smooth trail winds its way through the woods to a viewpoint of Ship Harbor. The trail then gently descends to the water, where there's an interpretive display about mudflats, home to soft-shell clams, marine worms, periwinkles, and a variety of crustaceans. This location is a great place to look for wading birds, such as sandpipers and lesser yellowlegs, which pick through the water and mud for food.

The interpretive displays along the trail were illustrated by Logan Parsins, a high school art teacher and freelance illustrator from California who is known for her detailed and colorful depictions of the natural world. In each display along the Ship Harbor Nature Trail, Parsins has illustrated the surrounding environment, including many of the creatures and plants you might come across.

Eventually, the trail leads to the center of the figure eight, a four-way intersection. There you can either head back to the trailhead on the forest portion of the easy loop, or continue on to the second loop, which travels over uneven terrain to some stunning outlooks on the rocky shore. On this section of the trail, small children may need assistance while walking over rocks and narrow bog bridges.

At the far end of the figure eight, you'll come to an interpretive display about tidal pools and the many creatures living therein. Nearby, just beyond a ledge of rosy granite, are several tidal pools to explore.

Small sea ducks called buffleheads are seen offshore from the Ship Harbor Nature Trail. In this photo, there are two males and one female.

My husband Derek and our dog Oreo, follow the Ship Harbor Nature Trail along the coast.

The Ship Harbor Nature Trail is accessible in the winter and makes a good snow-shoeing destination, but keep in mind that ice often makes the trail dangerous. Wear snowshoes or ice cleats when necessary, and factor in the short daylight hours. Always bring a headlamp, just in case.

The park asks that hikers stay on the trail; enjoy wildlife from a distance; and leave plants, rocks, and sea animals where you find them.

For more information: Visit www.nps/gov/acad or call (207) 288-3338.

Personal note: It was a surprise to see an empty parking area on a Saturday late in November when I arrived at the trailhead of Ship Harbor Nature Trail with my husband Derek and our dog Oreo. We're used to sharing Acadia National Park with plenty of other visitors, but during the off-season the park is much less crowded. It was a luxury to have the popular trail all to ourselves—at least for a little while.

After about 15 minutes on the easy trail, we paused so I could photograph a view of the grey-blue ocean under an overcast sky. As I fiddled with my camera settings to pick up the glow of sun filtering through the clouds, Oreo barked to announce a small group of hikers coming up behind us. We waved and let them pass. They were the first of several hikers that ended up passing us on the trail that day. We were moving slowly, as usual, largely due to my frequent stops to photograph the rosy granite shore.

Then I spotted a group of buffleheads—shy sea ducks that I rarely have the oppor-tunity to observe—and our hike came to a screaming halt. From our vantage point on a small cliff, I watched a bufflehead twist his big white head around to groom the dark iridescent feathers on his back. He then thrashed around in the water, flapping his wings and rolling on his side to groom his white chest with his salmon-colored

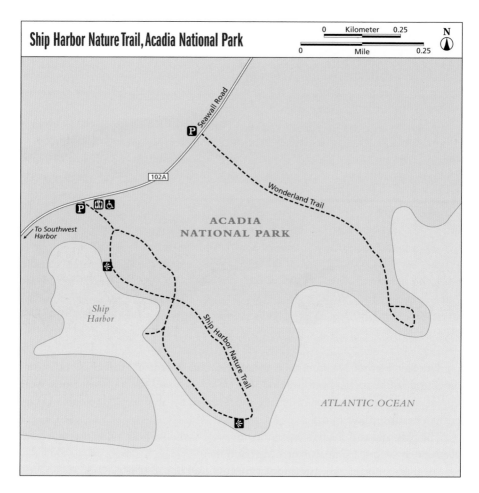

Ship Harbor Nature Trail, Acadia National Park

Kilometer
0 — 0.25
Mile
0 — 0.25

N

Seawall Road

102A

Wonderland Trail

ACADIA
NATIONAL PARK

To Southwest
Harbor

Ship
Harbor

Ship Harbor Nature Trail

ATLANTIC OCEAN

feet. I say "he" because the females and males of the group were easy to tell apart—the females having a different pattern with less white and none of the purple-blue iridescence to their dark feathers. (In the bird world, females are often less flashy, but if you look closely, their feathers often have a more intricate pattern, which helps them blend into their environment when they nest.)

The cold air of early winter quickly turned my fingers pink, reminding me that mitten season had begun. Nevertheless, Oreo waded into a frigid tidal pool. I let him splash around for a bit, but when he started drinking the salt water, I pulled him back to dry land. Briny vomit is on the list of things I don't want on the backseat of my car.

By the end of our hike, we were cold and ready for a hot meal, but if we'd been ambitious, we could have traveled just 0.3 mile down the road to the nearby Wonderland Trail, another great option for families in Acadia National Park. Also with a parking lot off 102A, the 1.4-mile Wonderland Trail is an easy hike through a whimsical habitat of granite and twisted pitch pines, ending at beaches covered with sand, seashells, seaweed gardens, and tidal pools.

Hike 5: Birdsacre, Stanwood Wildlife Sanctuary, in Ellsworth

About these trails: The Stanwood Wildlife Sanctuary, more commonly known as Birdsacre, is a 200-acre piece of quiet woodland surrounded by the hustle and bustle of downtown Ellsworth. The sanctuary includes a trail network, a bird rehabilitation facility, a nature center, and the 19th-century homestead of Cordelia J. Stanwood (1865–1958), a naturalist, ornithologist, wildlife photographer, and writer who lived and studied on the property for many years.

Difficulty: Easy to moderate. Birdsacre is home to a vast network of trails that are well signed and marked. The Perimeter Trail, marked with white blazes, is the longest trail in the network at 2 miles. Throughout the trail network, expect some exposed tree roots, rocky areas, and a few muddy sections.

Dogs: Permitted but should be kept away from the buildings and enclosures where injured birds are kept. Visitors are expected to pick up after their dogs and dispose of waste properly.

Cost: Admission is free, but donations can be made at the kiosk by the parking area and at www.birdsacre.com.

Access: The trail network is open to the public during daylight hours year-round. The homestead museum and nature center are open June through September, 10 a.m. to 4 p.m., dependent on volunteers. Trails are for foot traffic only. Bikes are not allowed.

Wheelchair accessibility: Birdsacre is home to a wheelchair-accessible woodland boardwalk, as well as a network of woodland trails that are not designed to be wheelchair accessible but travel over fairly even terrain and may be accessible to certain types of wheelchairs.

Hunting: Not permitted.

Restrooms: Available in the Richmond Nature Center, not far from the main parking lot. These restrooms are available only when the nature center is open, which is typically 10 a.m. to 4 p.m. June through September, dependent on volunteers.

How to get there: Birdsacre is located at 289 High Street (Route 3) in Ellsworth. Start at the four-way intersection of Main Street and High Street in Ellsworth and drive south on High Street (Route 1-Route 3) toward Bar Harbor. After about 1 mile, High Street (Route 3) splits off to the left from Route 1 and becomes a one-way road headed toward Bar Harbor. Take High Street (Route 3) and drive about 0.3 mile to Birdsacre on the right, just before the China Hill Restaurant.

GPS coordinates: 44.527908', -68.403503'

The daughter of a sea captain and prosperous merchant, Cordelia Stanwood was raised as a Victorian lady, yet she was determined to set her own course. Ignoring social expectations and dodging marriage, she devoted her life to studying nature at her childhood home, Birdsacre. Through her extensive studies of birds, she became one of the first highly respected female ornithologists and bird photographers.

Today, the nonprofit organization Birdsacre strives to keep alive Stanwood's passion for the study of nature and conservation.

Signs displaying quotes by ornithologist Cordelia Stanwood (1865–1958) are posted throughout the Birdsacre trail nework.

Year-round, Birdsacre visitors can trace Stanwood's footsteps on the sanctuary's system of footpaths, which consists of a 2-mile Perimeter Trail and many shorter trails that crisscross through woods and wetlands. It was on those trails that Stanwood spent many of her days observing birds and recording her findings in research notebooks and later, by camera (an Eastman Kodak No. 5 glass-plate camera, to be specific).

On wooden plaques posted on tree trunks throughout the trail network are quotes from Stanwood's field notes. These passages offer glimpses of her deep reverence for the wilderness, her love of animals, and the peace and happiness she found in being outdoors.

One such plaque reads: "Intimacy with nature is acquired slowly. It comes not with one year out of doors, or with two. You look and listen, bewail your stupidity, feel that you have acquired little new information; yet, are determined never to despair or give up. All at once you know what you never dreamed you knew before."

Through her studies Stanwood uncovered a wealth of information concerning bird behavior, life stages, and physiology. Her discoveries were published in popular magazines at the time, including the Audubon Society's "*Bird Lore.*" She also contributed to major publications, including Arthur Bent's *North American Birds* for the Smithsonian, and Edward Forbush's three-volume *Birds of Massachusetts and Other New England States.*

As you explore the Birdsacre trail network, you'll come upon the same landmarks that Stanwood enjoyed more than half a century ago—a boulder called "Egg Rock,"

A footpath in Birdsacre is bathed in sunlight.

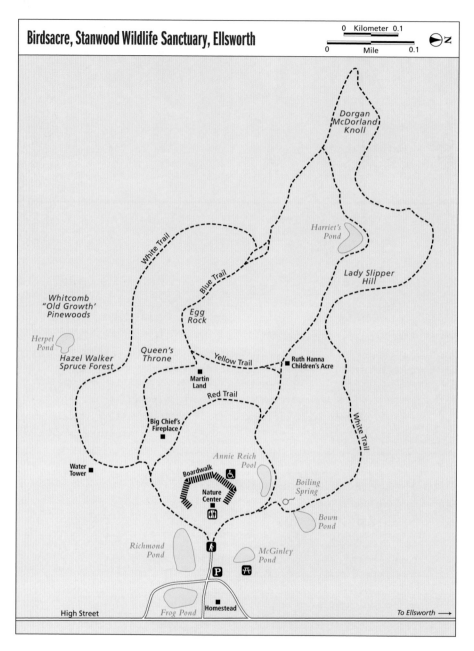

Birdsacre, Stanwood Wildlife Sanctuary, Ellsworth

0   Kilometer   0.1

0   Mile   0.1

N

Dorgan McDorland Knoll

Harriet's Pond

White Trail

Blue Trail

Lady Slipper Hill

Whitcomb "Old Growth' Pinewoods

Egg Rock

Herpel Pond

Hazel Walker Spruce Forest

Queen's Throne

Yellow Trail

Ruth Hanna Children's Acre

Martin Land

Red Trail

White Trail

Big Chief's Fireplace

Annie Reich Pool

Water Tower

Boardwalk

Boiling Spring

Nature Center

Bown Pond

Richmond Pond

McGinley Pond

P

Homestead

High Street

Frog Pond

To Ellsworth →

a giant white pine called "Queen's Throne," and several small ponds. Signs throughout the trail network direct hikers to these natural features. There are also signs that tell hikers about how many minutes it will take them to walk back "home," to the parking lots, Richmond Nature Center, Stanwood Museum, and a village of enclosures for various birds, including owls, hawks, geese, and ducks.

Flowers frame the sign for the Stanwood Homestead, the 19th-century home of Cordelia Stanwood.

Many of the birds housed at Birdsacre are being rehabilitated to be released back into the wild. But some of the birds at the sanctuary are nonreleasable, meaning they can't survive in the wilderness for one reason or another. For these birds, Birdsacre is their permanent home, and many of them have been trained to participate in educational nature programs.

The Richmond Nature Center, built by the Ellsworth Vocational Tech class in 1990, showcases a collection of bird and mammal mounts, many of them being more than 100 years old. The nature center also contains the Merrit Fitch egg collection, 58 species of eggs collected by two teenage boys in 1888.

Beside the nature center is the start to the Woodland Gardens and Boardwalk, a 540-foot-long wheelchair-accessible boardwalk that travels through five diverse environments. The project was proposed by the Master Gardener Volunteers of Hancock County in 1997 and was completed in 2001 with funding from several organizations and donors.

For more information: Visit www.birdsacre.com or call (207) 667-8460.

Personal note: I first visited Birdsacre during the winter of 2011. My mission was to check out the trail network, but when I first arrived, I was sidetracked by the many large buildings clustered near the parking area. Knowing the place to be a bird rehab center, I figured I might be able to spy some birds, and I can't recall any time I ever passed up being able to see an animal. So, with snow crunching underfoot, I approached one of the large buildings and looked through a big screen window. But I couldn't see a thing; it was too dark. Cupping my hands around my eyes to keep out the white light of winter, I leaned forward until my face nearly touched the screen, and my heart leapt with surprise. Staring back at me with a pair of wide, yellow eyes was a great horned owl—easily identifiable by its great size and long ear tufts (or horns).

Not wanting to disturb the bird, I backed away and decided it was time to hit the trails. What I recall from that visit was the quiet of the frozen forest, with only the occasional song of a black-capped chickadee or the muffled sound of snow falling from a tree to break the silence. I also recall visiting the "Queen's Throne," a giant white pine tree with roots and a trunk large enough to make a comfortable seat, and McGinley Pond, where injured ducks and geese live together in harmony, fed by Birdsacre staff and volunteers.

Aside from the birds, I didn't encounter another soul during that visit.

When I returned to the sanctuary four years later, in August 2015, much was different. The sign to the homestead museum was crowded by big yellow flowers, and the door was open. A group of children was gathered around a large carved map of the trail network, choosing the next route they'd take—the blue trail or the red trail. And a caretaker was walking around in a well-worn Birdsacre T-shirt, chatting with visitors and tending the birds.

Yet many things had remained the same. As I struck out on the nature trails, they were just as peaceful as I remembered them being. Instead of snow piles and icicles, the forest was adorned with ferns and lichens, mushrooms and moss, and the ponds were nearly hidden by the tall grasses and cattails that grew along their banks.

For that visit I'd brought along my dog Oreo, who tugged and tugged on his leash until I allowed him to wade into Harriet's Pond and cool off. We walked the whole trail network, which ended up being quite a workout and a test of the mind, as there are many intersecting trails blazed with different colors—white, yellow, blue, and red. We may have gotten briefly lost a couple times, coming upon a landmark we'd already seen but had not necessarily expected to see again.

Eventually, we made it out of the woods and back to the parking lot, where I left Oreo in the air-conditioned car while I visited the bird enclosures to marvel at red-tailed hawks and barred owls. I then wandered down to McGinley Pond, where I was growled at by a goose. Then, to my surprise, a seemingly flightless crow hopped up to the fence and started begging me for food with a high-pitched screech. I quickly retreated, feeling a bit guilty for causing such a hubbub.

Hike 6: Birch Point Discovery Trail in Steuben

About this trail: The Birch Point Discovery Trail is one of two interpretive hiking trails located on the 2,166-acre Petit Manan Point Division of the Maine Coastal Island National Wildlife Refuge Complex. Managed by the US Fish and Wildlife Service, the complex consists of 47 offshore islands and three coastal parcels of land, which all together total more than 7,400 acres.

Difficulty: Easy to moderate. The hike is a little more than 4 miles, round trip, and travels over fairly even terrain. Most of the trail is wide and smooth. At the far end of the hike, there is a short trail to Lobster Point and a small loop trail to Birch Point; both are narrow and require more attention to footing.

Dogs: Permitted if on a leash no longer than 10 feet. Visitors are expected to pick up after their dogs and dispose of waste properly.

Cost: Free.

Access: The trail is open year-round during daylight hours only. Snowmobiles, all-terrain vehicles, and open fires are not allowed.

Wheelchair accessibility: This trail is not constructed to be wheelchair accessible. It includes a number of narrow bog bridges and other obstacles.

Hunting: Parts of the refuge are open to hunting. Contact the refuge office for a list of open areas and current regulations.

Restrooms: None.

How to get there: Take Pigeon Hill Road (which turns into Petit Manan Point Refuge Road) off Route 1 in Steuben and follow it to the end. The parking area for the Birch Point Discovery Trail is 5.8 miles from Route 1. A parking area for the nearby Hollingsworth Trail is 6.2 miles from Route 1.

GPS coordinates: 44.439205', -67.893454'

If explored in its entirety, Birch Point Discovery Trail is about a 4-mile hike and leads hikers through a wide variety of habitats, including jack pine stands, coastal raised heath peatlands, blueberry barrens, old hay fields, fresh and saltwater marshes, cedar swamps, granite shores, and cobble beaches. Along the way are beautiful wooden displays that provide information about various flora and fauna on the property. There are also several chairs and benches located along the trail so you can stop, rest, and enjoy the beautiful scenery.

Starting in a blueberry field, where you are welcome to handpick blueberries for your own personal consumption, the Birch Point Discovery Trail winds through the field to enter a mixed forest. After about 0.8 mile, most of it in the forest, a side trail leads to the shore to a viewpoint of Carrying Place Cove. There you'll find a rest area, complete with Adirondack chairs and an interpretive sign about why coves are important to animals such as seabirds.

One of the key objectives of refuge management is to restore and manage colonies of nesting seabirds. The islands in the refuge complex provide habitat for terns, puffins, razorbills, black guillemots, Leach's storm-petrels, laughing gulls, common

The trail includes several narrow bog bridges.

Wooden interpretive displays are located along the trail, offering information about the landscape.

eiders, wading birds, and bald eagles. The mainland divisions provide habitat for songbirds, shorebirds, and waterfowl.

From the viewpoint of Carrying Place Cove, the trail leads back into the forest and travels another 0.7 mile, then splits. If you turn right, you'll hike 0.3 mile to an overlook on Lobster Point. Along the way you will pass a salt marsh (and interpretive sign about it) and cross over some bog bridges before reaching the end of the trail at a viewpoint and chairs by the water. On the other hand, if you turn left at the split in the trail, you will hike to a 0.7-mile loop on Birch Point that leads to several views of the water and crosses a cobblestone beach, which hikers can learn more about from an interpretive display by the shore.

If you'd like to extend your visit to the refuge, you can also hike the nearby Hollingsworth Trail, which is 1.8 miles round trip and similar in difficulty, leading through a variety of habitats on its way to the shore.

For more information: Call the refuge complex headquarters in Milbridge at (207) 546-2124 or visit www.fws.gov/refuge/maine_coastal_islands.

Personal note: The blueberries were just ripening in the field beyond the trailhead late in July when I arrived to walk Birch Point Discovery Trail for the first time. As I knelt down in the hot sun, I saw that some of the tiny berries were still a light shade of green, not yet ready to be picked, while others were violet, still young and tart. Then there were the ripe berries, deep blue, some so dark they appeared almost black. Those were ready to be eaten, and I did just that, plucking them carefully from their bushes and plopping them straight into my mouth.

Blueberries are ripe in the field at the start of the Birch Point Discovery Trail in August.

There's something about eating berries straight from the bush that makes me feel especially close to nature. It also brings me back to my childhood, when I so often used to pick wild berries from various locations around my house. I knew where everything was. The raspberries grew in a great patch across the road (technically on my neighbors' land, but they gave us permission), and wild strawberries grew along our driveway and in our backyard in early spring. I remember snacking on them as I waited for the school bus in the morning.

Then there was this huge blackberry patch near the hunting camp my family used to vacation at on Islesboro, an island off the coast of Maine. Once when I was a little girl, I became so excited about picking blackberries from that patch that I didn't pay proper attention and ended up "picking" a bumblebee that was busy collecting nectar from a blossom. It stung me, of course. My thumb. And I ran back to camp with tears running down my face. I remember my dad taking a look, making sure the stinger was out, and putting the whole traumatic event in perspective for me. Could I really blame the bee for stinging me? he asked me. After all, I'd tried to pick and eat it. At that, my tears were replaced by laughter.

Back on the Birch Point Discovery Trail, I was surprised at the unique interpretive displays dispersed along the trail. I'd seen plenty of educational displays before, but none designed like these. Each display is a carved wooden cubby containing three weatherproof "cards" that slide out so they can be read one at a time. Each card is set up similarly, with a photograph and a paragraph explaining an aspect of the immediate surroundings. For example, one display at the edge of a field contains signs

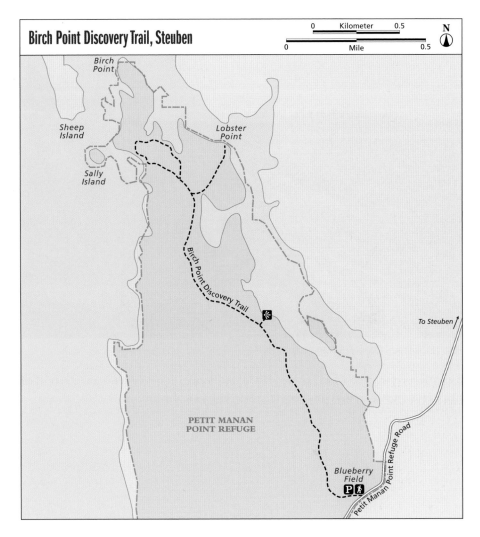

0   Kilometer   0.5   N

0   Mile   0.5

explaining that the refuge burns or mows several fields every three to five years so that they remain fields, which are a good habitat for ground-nesting birds. Otherwise, the fields would quickly grow up to become forestland.

As I explored the trail, I noted how well maintained and easy to follow it was, and I also paused to admire the long, winding boardwalks and bog bridges that kept my feet dry in the forest. It must have taken someone a long time to construct those bridges out in the woods.

At the far end of the hike, where the Birch Point Loop visits the shore, I sat on a boulder encrusted with bright orange-yellow lichen and took in the view, which seemed at the moment so idyllic to me, so picturesque. Hanging from weathered trees along the shore, stray lobster buoys swayed in the breeze. Light green grass rippled above the rocky beach and mounds of brown seaweed. And there I was, alone and

The Birch Point Discovery Trail leads to the rocky shore and stunning views of the ocean.

happy, feeling that the whole scene existed just for me, or better yet, I was a part of all that beauty, just a creature in the wilderness, enjoying the sun.

Hike 7 : Trenton Community Trail in Trenton

About this trail: Trenton Community Trail is a woodland footpath that officially opened to the public in the spring of 2013, and is maintained by the Trenton Parks and Recreation Committee, with assistance from the nonprofit group Friends of Acadia. The trail, which offers a hike that is just under 2.5 miles long, is shaped like a lollipop, starting out as one trail, then splitting into a loop.

Difficulty: Easy to moderate. The entire hike, including the bog boardwalk, is 2.4 miles. Watch your steps on the trail's many narrow bog bridges, and watch out for exposed tree roots and uneven ground.

Dogs: Permitted but must be kept under control at all times. Visitors are expected to pick up after their dogs and dispose of waste properly.

Cost: Free.

Access: The trail is open from dawn to dusk, year-round.

Wheelchair accessibility: The trail is not constructed to be accessible to wheelchairs or strollers. The terrain is uneven and the trail includes many narrow bog bridges.

Hunting: Permitted.

Restrooms: None.

How to get there: A large paved parking area for the trail is located at the end of Gateway Center Drive, which is on the west side of Route 3 in Trenton. To get there from Ellsworth, start where Route 1-Route 3 split and take Route 3 south toward Mount Desert Island. Drive for about 4.9 miles to Gateway Center Drive, a wide paved road that will be on your right. Proceed to the parking area at the end of the drive, at the turnaround. The trail kiosk and trailhead are visible from the parking area.

GPS coordinates: 44.467634', -68.374656'

From the trailhead kiosk, the trail enters the forest immediately and leads over a series of bog bridges, as well as two footbridges that span scenic brooks. At 0.5 mile the trail splits into a loop, which is 1.2 miles long.

Much of this trail travels through a wet, whimsical forest, with moss carpeting the forest floor and reaching up tree trunks. Along the way you'll come to a nice quiet resting place by a brook, where two Adirondack chairs are available for visitors to sit on.

Along the trail you'll come across colorful and detailed educational displays about the wildlife and plant life of the area. Also, the Hancock County Master Gardener Volunteers have started labeling plants, from the highbush blueberry bushes near the trailhead to the stunted black spruce trees in the bog. The small metal labels blend in with the environment, so you'll have to keep your eyes peeled.

At the far end of the loop trail is a short spur trail that leads to a wide, wooden boardwalk. This boardwalk takes visitors out into a native dwarf shrub bog to an observation platform with educational displays about the habitat. Out and back, this adds 0.2 mile to your hike.

The main trail is marked with blue blazes painted on trees, while this spur trail to the bog boardwalk is marked with white blazes. It's important to follow these trail

At the far end of the loop trail is a long bog boardwalk that leads to a platform in a bog with benches and interpretive displays.

markers, as several woods roads cross the trail, especially near the trailhead. For example, not far from the trailhead, the trail appears to fork at the "Trenton Community Forest" sign. The left path is actually an old woods road that reconnects to the trail farther along. (Visitors are welcome to explore it.) The right path is the actual trail, marked with blue blazes.

Construction of the Trenton Community Trail was made possible by funding from the Davis Conservation Fund, Friends of Acadia, National Parks Conservation Association, Nature Valley, and the Yawkey Foundation. The Trenton Community Trail Committee and hundreds of volunteers contributed thousands of hours of trail work to create this outdoor destination for the community.

For more information: Call the Trenton Town Office at (207) 667-7207 or visit http://friendsofacadia.org, where a trail map is available.

Personal note: I adopted my dog Oreo in the spring of 2013, right around my birthday, and ever since, he's been accumulating a wardrobe, which includes a hiking pack, a variety of collars and harnesses, and several jackets. I know what you're thinking: Poor dog. But for the most part, Oreo's wardrobe really is about practicality.

Early on, I realized that Oreo has a hard time keeping warm. He's a pit bull mix, with short black and white fur that altogether vanishes on his stomach and chest. That leaves him vulnerable to the cold and abrasive underbrush. But the problem with buying Oreo protective clothing is that he's not the typical dog shape, if there is such a thing. He's got a big head, thick neck, and round chest, paired with rather short legs and a tiny waist. So finding stuff that fits him is difficult. Fortunately, I found a local woman who makes custom dog clothing (Dogn'i of Bangor). So Oreo now has two custom fleece jackets and several overcoats to keep him warm in the winter.

Bundled up in one of these fleece jackets (the classic lumberjack plaid one, to be specific), and with his paws protected with Musher's Secret (a wax that protects dog paws against cold and abrasive surfaces), Oreo joined me to explore Trenton Community Trail in December, on a day with a predicted high of 35 degrees with a wind chill that lowered that to 20 degrees. I packed an extra dog jacket, just in case.

As we walked through the beautiful mossy woods of the forest, I was pleased to notice that Oreo seemed completely comfortable—no shivering or whining. He did, however, roll and thrash about on the ground when I stopped to take photos of the trail. I think this odd behavior may be his canine way of getting attention, or expressing impatience.

The bog bridges helped keep us out of the frigid puddles and brooks. And the boardwalk at the far end of the loop was a great "end" destination, with three interpretive signs and four benches for visitors to rest on while taking the view of the bog.

While only patches of snow covered the ground that day, I imagine the trail would be a great place to go snowshoeing. The blue blazes mark the trees regularly, making it an easy route to follow, even in the winter when the snow can make trails more difficult to see.

Trenton Community Trail, Trenton

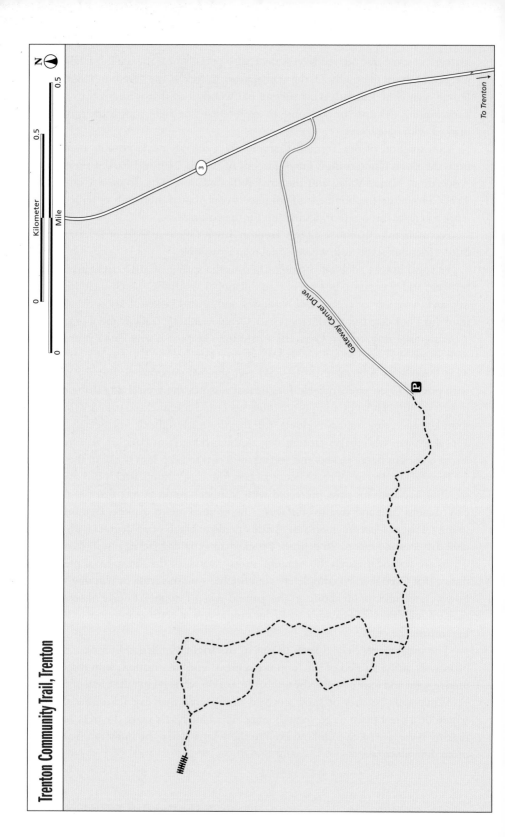

A wooden bridge crosses over a brook on the trail.

My favorite spot on the trail was the bridge spanning the second brook from the trailhead. The swiftly flowing water, bordered by mossy banks, appeared reddish orange in the sunlight. I'm not sure why. Sometimes it's nice to just accept nature's beauty for what it is. It's a peaceful place, and I imagine that's why the trail crew placed two wooden chairs in the woods nearby.

Hike 8: Beech Hill Preserve in Rockport

About these trails: Atop Beech Hill in Rockport, surrounded by blueberry fields, stands a beautiful old stone building called Beech Nut. Its sod roof sprouts grass and fresh wildflowers each spring, and from its stone veranda, you can see across the forest to the glittering water of Penobscot Bay, the rolling Camden Hills, and the Saint George Peninsula. Two public trails lead to this beautiful vista and historic structure.

Difficulty: Easy. The 0.75-mile Summit Road Trail is wide and smooth much of the way, though there is a rocky section not far from the trailhead. This trail leads through the blueberry fields, meaning it is open to the sun and wind much of the way. The Woods Loop Trail is just under a mile long, making for a 2-mile hike, round trip. Much of the trail is in the woods, sheltered from the elements.

Dogs: Permitted but must be on leash at all times. Visitors are expected to pick up after their dogs and dispose of waste properly.

Cost: Free, but donations to support the property can be made at www.coastalmountains.org/donate.

Access: Open during daylight hours. Vehicles, bicycles, horses, fires, and camping are not allowed on the preserve. And groups larger than 12 should obtain permission before visiting.

Wheelchair accessibility: The trails were not constructed to be wheelchair accessible.

Hunting: Permitted in the forested areas only.

Restrooms: There is a portable toilet near the top of Beech Hill, beside Beech Nut, from June through September.

How to get there: There are two trailheads to the trail network of Beech Hill Preserve.

To start on the Summit Road Trail, the first and original trail of the preserve, drive to Rockport on Route 1 and turn onto Beech Hill Road, which is across from Hoboken Gardens. (Beech Hill Road will be on the right if you are heading south.) Drive about a mile on Beech Hill Road and the parking area is on the left, just past the old gate to Beech Hill and a stone wall.

To start on the Woods Loop Trail, drive to Rockport on Route 1 and turn onto Rockville Street. (If you are heading south, it will be the first right after Fresh Off the Farm.) Drive about 0.7 mile on Rockville Street and the parking area is on the right.

GPS coordinates: 44.170070', -69.107441'

The building—known as Beech Nut—was constructed in the early 1900s by the Gribbel family to be a spot for picnics and afternoon tea. The architect hired to design and construct Beech Nut was Norway native Hans O. Heistad, who moved to Maine in 1905 to work on Bar Harbor's coastal estates. His design for Beech Nut was inspired by the traditional Norwegian mountain house design of his childhood, known as a hytter. The building's stones, individually wrapped in burlap, were hauled to the site by horse and set in place by hand.

Constructed atop the hill, this highly visible stone structure has inspired a variety of stories over the years, from rumors that it was a German spy house during World War I to tales about the site's mystical properties.

In 1986 Beech Hill was protected by a conservation easement, and in 2003 the Coastal Mountains Land Trust purchased the summit of the hill—including Beech

A historic stone building known as Beech Nut stands atop Beech Hill. Visitors often spend time on the stone veranda of the building, enjoying the views of the region.

Nut—with support from the Land for Maine's Future program, the MBNA Foundation, and individual donors. The following year, the building (and surrounding property) was listed on the National Register of Historic Places in the State of Maine.

Today, Beech Hill and Beech Nut are a part of the Beech Hill Preserve, 300 acres of land managed for grassland bird habitat, organic blueberry production, and scenic and historic preservation values. This preserve is home to two easy hiking trails, both of which culminate at the top of Beech Hill at Beech Nut.

The Summit Road Trail is the original trail on the property and begins at the Beech Hill Road trailhead. First it follows an old stone wall, then an old farm road for an easy, 0.75-mile hike to the summit of Beech Hill. Along the way are educational displays about the grassland habitat and the land's blueberry operation.

The Woods Loop begins at the Rockville Street trailhead and passes through a 2-acre sugar maple stand and a young mixed forest before splitting into a loop. At the far end of the loop a single trail travels through blueberry fields and finishes the climb to the summit of Beech Hill.

In 2007 the Coastal Mountains Land Trust completed a full restoration of Beech Nut, which included replacement of the building's sod roof, windows, doors, and exterior veranda, as well as the repointing of the building's stonework. May through October, open houses are held twice a month for the public to explore the inside of the building, but if you show up on any other day, you can still learn a great deal about the history of Beech Nut from a detailed educational sign posted on the veranda.

My dog Oreo sniffs at the wildflowers beside the wide Summit Road Trail in the preserve.

The preserve is a popular place for wildlife watchers, being one of the official stops on the Maine Birding Trail, with more than 125 bird species on its checklist.

Visitors to the property are asked to stay on trails. The fields are managed for grassland bird habitat and organic blueberry production that financially helps support the preserve, and the forested areas are home to a variety of wildlife. Removal of vegetation is strictly prohibited, but visitors may pick blueberries along the side of the trail without crossing the string fence. Also, visitors are allowed on the fields to pick blueberries during an annual Free Pick event, announced each year on the Coastal Mountains Land Trust website.

For more information: Visit www.coastalmountains.org or call (207) 236-7091.

Personal note: A number of friends encouraged me to visit the unusual stone "hut" atop Beech Hill, and on June 30, 2013, I took their advice and traveled to Rockport with my then boyfriend (now husband) Derek and our dog Oreo.

We took our time on the Summit Road Trail, soaking in the sun and admiring common wildflowers—daisies, beach rose, black-eyed Susans, and fireweed. And after reading an educational sign about the native wood lily, we successfully sought it out, too. Swaying on tall green stalks, the deep orange blossoms were scattered throughout the fields.

While the blackflies and mosquitoes were thick in the forest, they didn't bother us much in the sunny fields. We did, however, observe a number of other insects, including bumblebees, and a bright yellow spider called a goldenrod crab spider.

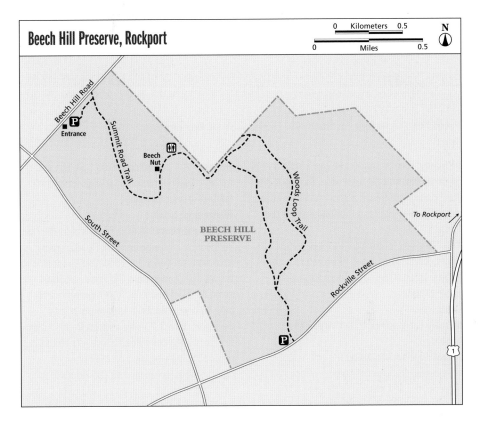

Beech Nut, its sod roof adorned with yellow wildflowers, was much grander than I anticipated, with a spacious stone veranda wrapping around three sides of the locked building. There on the summit of the hill, we lingered for a while, reading educational displays about Beech Nut and peeking in its windows into a room with a large table that is likely used for public programs. Looking out over the blueberry fields and the forests below, we could see all the way to the ocean.

Hike 9: Old Pond Railway Trail in Hancock

About this trail: The Old Pond Railway Trail follows nearly 3 miles of the former Maine Shoreline Railway, which was last traveled by train in the 1980s. A century ago, the railway was used to transport tourists from Brewer to Hancock's McNeil Point Ferry Landing on their way to the famous Bar Harbor.

Difficulty: Easy to moderate. The 3-mile trail is relatively flat, straight, and wide. The most difficult part of the trail is a short section between the old railway bed and the trailhead on Old Route 1.

Pets: Dogs are permitted but must be kept under control at all times. Visitors are expected to pick up after their dogs and dispose of waste properly.

Cost: Free.

Access: Fires, camping, and ATVs are not permitted.

Wheelchair accessibility: The trail is not constructed to be accessible by wheelchair. However, the first section of the trail is wide and straight, with just a few roots and rocks, and could be traversed by some off-road wheelchairs, depending on the model of wheelchair and the physical abilities of the wheelchair user.

Hunting: Not permitted on the trail, but the trail is closely bordered by private land where hunting may be practiced.

Restrooms: None.

How to get there: Most people access the trail by the east entrance off Point Road, across from Hancock Town Hall (because this trailhead is less than a mile from Old Pond, the most scenic area of the trail). To get there from the intersection of Route 1 and Route 182 in Hancock, drive 3.2 miles east on Route 1 and turn right onto Point Road. Drive less than 0.1 mile to the parking area on the right.

The west entrance is off Old Route 1. To get there from the intersection of Route 1 and Route 182 in Hancock, drive 0.7 mile east on Route 1 and turn right onto Old Route 1. Drive 0.4 mile to the parking area on the right.

GPS coordinates: 44.527804', -68.253959'

The wide footpath, which officially opened to the public in July 2012, travels along the abandoned railway's partially buried rails and moss-covered railway ties from Hancock Town Hall to Old Pond and on to Kilkenny Cove, passing through a quiet mixed forest. The straight, flat trail is a great option for an easy walk, and in the winter it's a good path for snowshoeing and cross-country skiing. It also serves local wormers and clammers, who use it to access the flats that form around Carrying Place Inlet, Old Pond, and Hills Cove.

The public has access to this trail thanks to three land conservation trusts, the town of Hancock, state organizations, and local volunteers. It all started in 2008, when nearly 3 miles of the old railway were acquired by the Crabtree Neck Land Trust, with the help of the Maine Coast Heritage Trust. A year later, three local Eagle Scouts constructed the parking area at the east entrance, cleared the first half mile of the trail, and repaired the trestle bridge at Old Pond, making it safe for visitors to cross. The bridge offers some of the most spectacular scenery of the hike.

Signs mark both the west and east entrance of the Old Pond Railway Trail.

Old Pond is a body of salt water near Carrying Place Inlet, which links Youngs Bay to Taunton Bay on the coast of Hancock. It's an excellent place for bird-watching and also frequented by seals, according to the Maine Coast Heritage Trust. Keep an eye out for bald eagles, ducks, geese, gulls, and in the fall, migrating warblers.

The trail continued to develop in 2010, when the Maine Coast Heritage Trust purchased a waterfront property at the western end of the trail with the assistance of Crabtree Neck Land Trust and a contribution from Land for Maine's Future. The Maine Coast Heritage Trust then transferred the property to Frenchman Bay Conservancy, which built the west entrance parking area and made trail improvements that completed the 3-mile trail.

Since the old rail bed doesn't lead directly to the west entrance on Old Route 1, the Frenchman Bay Conservancy had to do a bit of trail blazing. To reach the west entrance, the trail veers right, leaving the old rail bed, and climbs over a tangle of exposed roots. This short section of trail is narrow and travels over a number of bog bridges. Be sure to follow the trail blazes as the trail weaves through an enchanting cedar forest to the west trailhead.

For more information: Visit www.crabtreenecklandtrust.org, www.mcht.org, or www.frenchmanbay.org.

Personal note: Stubborn patches of snow and ice still covered the ground in the shaded woods of Hancock on April 12, 2014, when Derek (then boyfriend, now husband) and I first explored the Old Pond Railway Trail with our dog Oreo. We began our hike at the east entrance and walked to Old Pond, where the trail was

The trail crosses an old trestle bridge that was repaired by local Eagle Scouts.

sandwiched by salty water at nearly high tide. Seaweed rippled in the current that swept under the bridge. Granite blocks lined the shore on both sides. And the trail continued on a narrow sliver of land until it met a bridge with solid metal rails and wide planking. There we set our packs down to bask in the sun. Finally, it was starting to feel like spring.

Nearby, a group of four Canada geese eyed us warily, then seemed to relax, dipping their long necks underwater from time to time as they swam. Farther from us, a number of black-and-white ducks—common goldeneyes, perhaps—bobbed in the gentle waves, and a large group of gulls lounged on the grassy shore. Then, for a reason unknown to us, the gulls launched into the blue sky to wheel over our heads. On the bridge, we waited to be splattered with bird droppings that fortunately never came.

Past Old Pond, we traveled through a mixed forest scattered with boulders and a variety of tall, old trees. Tracing the old railway, the trail was fairly straight, so that even in the midst of a dense forest, we would see far ahead of us.

As we walked, I started to notice light-colored areas on tree trunks and exposed tree roots where the dark bark had recently been peeled off. Beavers and porcupines both do this, eating the nutritious inner layer of the bark. But beavers usually gnaw down the tree in the process. We didn't see any felled trees, and since we weren't around any substantial bodies of water, I concluded that it was a porcupine—or several—that was stripping the trees of their bark. From that point on, we kept Oreo on leash.

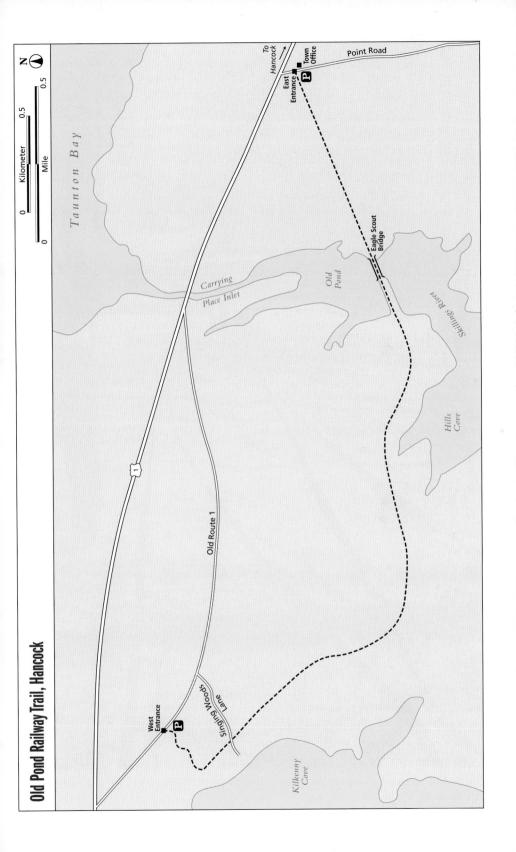

Old Pond Railway Trail, Hancock

N

Taunton Bay

Kilometer
0   0.5
0   0.5
Mile

Carrying
Place Inlet

Old Pond

To
Hancock

East
Entrance

Town
Office

P

Point Road

Eagle Scout
Bridge

Skillings River

Hills
Cove

1

Old Route 1

Singing Woods
Lane

West
Entrance

P

Kilkenny
Cove

The trail follows nearly 3 miles of the former Maine Shoreline Railway, which was last traveled by train in the 1980s.

A bit farther down the trail, we came across a porcupine den, burrowed into the muddy bank of a brook. It was surrounded by peanut-shaped droppings, which Oreo was quite excited about. But when he tried to stick his head into the den, we pulled him away and continued our hike, not wanting to deal with a muzzle full of sharp quills.

In all my time on Maine hiking trails over the years, porcupines are one of the creatures I've seen most often. And on a number of occasions, I've come across their dens. Sometimes the dens are in old hollow trees, while other times they are built into the ground or a jumble of boulders, and these dens always seem to be surrounded by droppings, which sometimes accumulate into enormous and, quite frankly, comical piles. I guess porcupines aren't the tidiest of housekeepers.

Hike 10: Moose Point State Park in Searsport

About these trails: Moose Point was given to the state of Maine for use as a state park in 1952 in memory of George A. Carver (1836–1908) by his heirs John A. H. Carver, Clifford M. Carver, and G. W. Douglas Carver. Today, wide, well-maintained trails wind throughout the wooded portion of the park, combining stunning ocean views and the beauty of a mature forest filled with towering white pines.

Difficulty: Easy. Exploring all trails in the park is about a 1.5-mile hike.

Dogs: Permitted but must be kept on a leash not exceeding 4 feet in length and attended to at all times. Visitors are expected to pick up after their dogs and dispose of waste properly.

Cost: Admission is $3 for adult Maine residents, $4 for adult nonresidents, $1 for senior nonresidents, $1 for children 5–11 years old, and free for senior (65+) Maine residents and children under 5 years old.

Access: The park gates are open 9 a.m. to sunset daily from Memorial Day to October 1, but the public is welcome to use the park during the off-season by parking outside the closed gates and walking in from there. Bikes are not permitted on trails.

Wheelchair accessibility: Some of the trails are generally accessible to wheelchairs. They meet most ADA standards but have a few barriers. People who use wheelchairs may need some assistance. The parking area and restrooms are wheelchair accessible, and there are wheelchair-accessible picnic tables by the main parking area.

Hunting: Not permitted between June 1 and Labor Day; permitted during the rest of the year, though the discharge of any weapon is prohibited from or within 300 feet of any picnic area, camping area or campsite, parking area, building, shelter, boat launch site, posted trail, or other developed area.

Restrooms: Available by the main parking area Memorial Day to October 1.

How to get there: The park is located off Route 1, between the downtown areas of Belfast and Searsport, with the address of 310 West Main Street in Searsport.

GPS coordinates: 44.435339', -68.944860'

George A. Carver was a ship captain and shipbuilder who sailed from Searsport in the late 1800s. His heirs also donated the Carver Memorial Library to the town of Searsport in 1908, fulfilling a long-held wish of the captain. The exterior of the library was built with fieldstones taken from the Carver Farm, on what today is Moose Point State Park. A day after the library's dedication ceremony in October 1910, the *Bangor Daily News* described the library as "a thing of beauty and a joy for generations of Searsport people to come."

Moose Point State Park is a popular place for local residents and people who are traveling along coastal Route 1. In addition to three easy hiking trails, the park features a playground, gazebo, group shelter, and many picnic tables and grills. By Penobscot Bay, two sets of stairs lead down to a rocky beach, which has patches of sand here and there. Benches are located near the water for people who just want to sit and enjoy the view.

Wooden steps lead down to a rocky beach at the park.

A red squirrel stands on a tree limb beside a trail at the park.

Benches are also located along the hiking trails—Big Spruce Trail, Moose Trail, and Meadow Trail—which are wide and level. These trails are great for families with small children, though parents and guardians should be mindful of where the forest slopes down to the beach.

Of the three trails, the Big Spruce Trail is probably the most traveled. From the main parking area, it moves through a quiet evergreen forest, tracing the shore at a distance. It then passes by an old apple orchard and arrives at a viewpoint by the water, where a bench is located. From there, the trail continues to trace the shore, intersecting with a park service road and visiting a large spruce tree before ending at Moose Trail.

Moose Trail is completely in the forest, without any ocean views. Since there are a lot more deciduous trees located along this trail, it would be an especially beautiful trail to walk in the autumn, when leaves are changing colors. Also along this trail are scenic footbridges and two benches. One end of the trail is at the park road, near the entrance station, and the other end is at the service road, near the restrooms.

The Meadow Trail is across the park road from the other two trails. Starting by the park entrance station, it travels through a meadow, around the group shelter and gazebo, to the shore, where stairs lead down to the beach.

If interested in geology, you can take a self-guided tour of the park's geological features with a packet produced by the Maine Geological Survey, available online at www.maine.gov/moosepoint. Most of the sites highlighted in the tour are located along the shoreline adjacent to the park's Big Spruce Trail. The trail weaves through

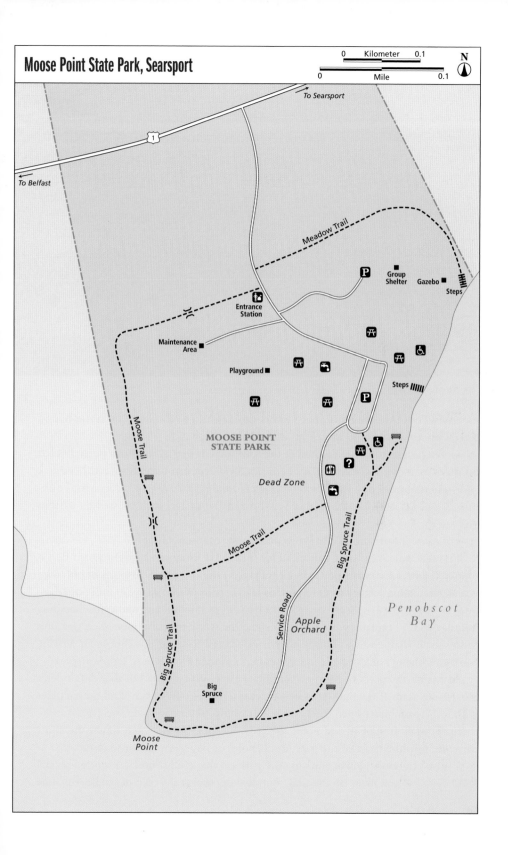

Moose Point State Park, Searsport

To Searsport

To Belfast

Meadow Trail

P

Group Shelter

Gazebo

Steps

Entrance Station

Maintenance Area

Playground

Steps

P

Moose Trail

MOOSE POINT STATE PARK

Dead Zone

?

Moose Trail

Big Spruce Trail

Service Road

Apple Orchard

Penobscot Bay

Big Spruce Trail

Big Spruce

Moose Point

The Big Spruce Trail traces the shore, leading to views of the water.

the forest above the shoreline, but visitors can descend to the shore from the trail in several places to view the sites. This is best done at low tide.

Geological features highlighted in the tour include glacial striations (scratches left on rocks by moving glaciers), glacial erratics (boulders that differ from local bedrock and were transported to the beach by glaciers), and glacial till (a heterogeneous mixture of pulverized rock debris that was carried by glaciers and released by various processes).

For more information: Visit www.maine.gov/moosepoint or call (207) 548-2882.

Personal note: On Saint Patrick's Day in 2013, I threw on a bright green fleece, topped it with a fuzzy, maroon windproof jacket, and drove to Searsport, an old town with a fascinating history as the home of sea captains. With nearly 10 miles of coastline on Penobscot Bay, Searsport used to have a big shipbuilding and cargo handling industry, and sea captains who traveled around the world brought home their treasures to the small Maine town. This history is celebrated today at the Penobscot Marine Museum, Maine's oldest maritime museum, located just off Route 1 in Searsport.

In March the gates of Moose Point State Park were closed, but that didn't deter me. Maine State Parks trails are open to visitors year-round, even if all the facilities within the park aren't open (such as the restrooms). All I had to do was park outside the gate, walk around it, and enter the park by foot. As I walked down the short driveway into the heart of the park, the Penobscot Bay glittered ahead of me.

I wasn't the only person enjoying the park on that chilly Sunday. I spotted several families and solo walkers on the trails, bundled up against the cold ocean breeze. The temperature was in the low 30s, but in some spots in the forest, where the trees broke the wind and the sun filtered through, the day felt much warmer.

A couple walking along the Old Spruce Trail saw my camera and paused to tell me about a young bald eagle they often see perching in the tall evergreens that lean out toward the shore. I looked for the bird as I walked slowly along the trail, even backtracking a few times, but I didn't catch sight of it. I did, however, see a hairy woodpecker, golden-crowned kinglets, and plenty of red squirrels and crows.

Hike 11 : Shore Acres Preserve in Deer Isle

About these trails: Shore Acres Preserve is one of the many places hikers and wildlife watchers can explore on Deer Isle, a place that is known for its whimsical, mossy forests and stunning ocean scenes. With three trails forming a loop that is about 1.5 miles long and visits the shore in several spots, the preserve is an excellent place for people looking for a short but beautiful hike to the ocean.

Difficulty: Easy. The 1.5-mile loop trail travels over fairly even terrain to several scenic locations along the shore. The trail is well-traveled and marked with blazes. Be careful of exposed tree roots and rocks.
Dogs: Permitted but must be kept on leash. Visitors are expected to pick up after their dogs and dispose of waste properly.
Cost: Free.
Access: The preserve is open to day use only. Fires are prohibited. Groups over 12 in number must obtain permission from the Island Heritage Trust. The trails are designed for foot traffic only.

Wheelchair accessibility: The trail was not constructed to be wheelchair accessible. It contains an abundance of exposed tree roots and rocks.
Hunting: Permitted.
Restrooms: None.
How to get there: From Route 15 in Deer Isle, turn onto the Sunshine Road at Mill Pond Mobil. Drive 1.2 miles and bear left at the fork onto Greenlaw District Road. (Watch for traffic coming around the bend.) Drive about 0.9 mile to the parking area, which is on the right and marked with a sign.
GPS coordinates: 44.223726', -68.636303'

The preserve is owned and maintained by the Island Heritage Trust, a nonprofit organization working for the environmental and scenic protection of Deer Isle and Stonington.

From the gravel parking area of Shore Acres Preserve, a trail heads into the forest to a kiosk, where hikers can sign the trail register and leave comments about their experience. Brochures about the trail and the land trust are also available at the kiosk.

Continuing past the kiosk, the blue-blazed trail travels over a rocky area and soon reaches a fork, the beginning of a loop. Veer right to travel the loop counterclockwise, starting on the Stonewall Trail; or veer left to travel the loop clockwise, starting on the Goldthread Trail.

The Stonewall Trail, marked with blue blazes, travels through a mossy forest on a series of bog bridges and visits an old stone wall before leading to the shore, where you can take a right onto a side trail to a rocky beach. (Beware of a barbed wire fence that runs through the forest at the preserve's boundary line not far from this trail.)

Once at the shore, continue the loop hike on the Shore Trail, which is marked with orange blazes and traces the water through more open terrain. Prepare to encounter tall grass, underbrush, and raspberry bushes, which should remind you to check your body thoroughly for ticks after the walk. As the trail travels along the

A wading bird is seen on the shore of the preserve.

shore, there are several scenic outlooks and a few places you can access the rocky shore and water.

As you walk this trail, you'll see the bedrock exposed along the shore. The preserve lies on what is known as Oak Point Granite, one of the two granite bodies on Deer Isle. This pink-tinged rock crystallized approximately 370 million years ago, with its principal materials being reddish potassium feldspar, cream-colored sodium feldspar, and quartz, according to the preserve brochure produced by Island Heritage Trust.

Also described in the brochure are the landmarks seen from the shore of the preserve. Looking out from the preserve's rocky beaches, you'll see to your left (north) Oak Point, with Good Island in the foreground. To the right of that is Campbell Island, then White Island and several points and coves of Greenlaw Neck and Stinson Neck.

The Shore Trail leads to a letterbox—a wooden compartment nailed to a tree that contains a waterproof box, rubber stamp, and notebook used in an outdoor activity called letterboxing—then turns away from the shore to meet Goldthread Trail, which was named for the landscape's abundance of goldthread, a low-lying plant that produces delicate white flowers in the spring. This trail is also marked with orange blazes and travels through a forest filled with moss and ferns. It will lead you back to the beginning of the loop near the preserve trailhead.

The trails are maintained by volunteers of the Island Heritage Trust, which was founded by local residents in 1987. Since then, they have obtained conservation easements of more than 771 acres on Deer Isle and Stonington, protecting more than 13

Ferns and mosses cover the forest floor of the preserve in many places.

miles of shore. The trust has also taken ownership of 18 properties, including Mark Island, Settlement Quarry, and Shore Acres Preserve.

For more information: Call the Island Heritage Trust at (207) 348-2455, e-mail iht@islandheritagetrust.org, or visit www.islandheritagetrust.org.

Personal note: The island towns of Deer Isle and Stonington are home to several walking trails that are especially prized by bird-watchers. Some trails are open to dogs, and some aren't. So before driving to Deer Isle with my dog Oreo, I visited the Island Heritage Trust website to narrow down which trails would be open to my furry hiking companion.

We ended up with Shore Acres Preserve because, on such a nice, sunny day, I figured we'd be remiss not to visit the ocean. Right away, I could tell that the trails of the preserve were well traveled, but on that particular Friday, we ran into only one family of four while traveling the loop.

As I've spent more time hiking trails on Deer Isle, I've developed the opinion that the island has some of the most beautiful forests in Maine. Perhaps it's the moss, which forms in a thick carpet over the forest floor in so many places. Combined with the old weathered evergreens, ferns, and lichen, this landscape of so many shades of green is only further enhanced by the scent of the ocean, which sneaks in through the trees as you near the shore.

As Oreo and I picked our way along the Shore Trail, we paused several times to rest on the rosy sun-warmed granite. That day, the ocean seemed more green than

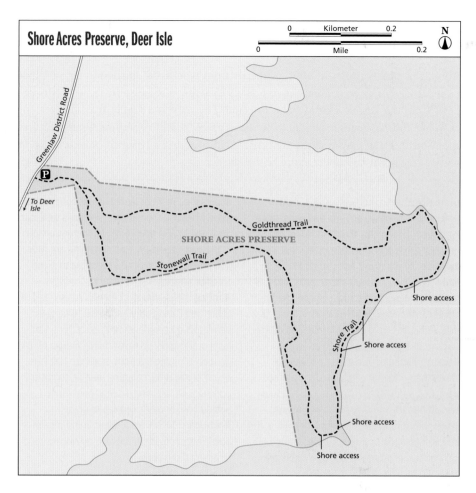

blue, sparkling in the sun. On a long leash, Oreo waded into the cold salt water, splashing with his paws and biting at the floating seaweed.

Hike 12: Lily Bay State Park on Moosehead Lake

About this trail: Created in 1961 primarily from woodland donated by Scott Paper Company, Lily Bay State Park encompasses 925 acres on the eastern shore of Moosehead Lake, the largest lake in New England. The park is a family friendly spot for camping, fishing, boating, paddling, picnicking, and wildlife watching. It also features a well-maintained easy walking trail that winds through a beautiful mixed forest to several viewpoints along the shore of the lake.

Difficulty: Easy to moderate. The 1.7-mile walking trail is mostly smooth and wide, making it great for families with small children. However, there is one section of the trail where the forest floor has not been smoothed out, and this section contains many rocks and tangles of exposed tree roots, making footing trickier. This more difficult section is about 0.4 mile and spans from the east trailhead at Rowell Cove to the first side trail to the shore.

Dogs: Permitted on trails if on a leash no longer than 4 feet at all times. Dogs are not permitted on the beach between April 1 and September 30, and they are never allowed inside the comfort station (a building along the trail with restrooms, showers, baby changing stations, and outdoor sinks). Visitors are expected to pick up after their dogs and dispose of waste properly.

Cost: Park admission is $4 for adult Maine residents, $6 for adult nonresidents, $2 for senior nonresidents, $1 for children 5–11 years old, and free for seniors (65+) and children under 5 years old.

Access: For day users the park is open 9 a.m. to sunset daily from Memorial Day through Columbus Day. In the winter the park gates are closed, but visitors are welcome to park outside the gates and enter the park on foot (or ski). About 5 miles of trails and park roads are groomed for cross-country skiing, and Moosehead Lake is a popular spot for ice-fishing.

Wheelchair accessibility: Parking, restrooms, and picnic tables in the park are wheelchair accessible. The boat launch is not constructed to be wheelchair accessible. The trails were not designed to ADA standards, but some sections of the trail, especially by Dunn Point, are wide and smooth and may be accessible to some types of wheelchairs.

Hunting: Not permitted between June 1 and Labor Day. During all other times, hunting is permitted in accordance with state laws and local ordinances. However, the discharge of any weapon is prohibited from or within 300 feet of any picnic area, camping area or campsite, parking area, building, shelter, boat launch site, posted trail, or other developed area.

Restrooms: Toilets are located in the park's comfort station. There are also outhouses throughout the park.

How to get there: From the traffic light at the center of downtown Greenville (at the intersection of Moosehead Lake Road, Pritham Avenue, and Lily Bay Road), take Lily Bay Road, which travels along the east side of Moosehead Lake. Follow Lily Bay Road for 13 miles and turn left onto State Park Road at the sign for Lily Bay State Park. A short way down the road, you'll pass through an entrance booth where you'll need to pay a small entrance fee. You can collect a park map there. Past the entrance booth, you'll come to a fork in the road. Bear left and follow the signs to the day parking area near the beach and boat landing on Dunn Point.

GPS coordinates: 45.568853', -69.538450'

Big Spencer Mountain is seen across Moosehead Lake from the beach at the park.

One of the most popular spots in the park is an open area on Dunn Point that includes a sandy beach, a playground, benches, and picnic tables scattered through a stand of pines. Nearby is a large boat launch with several wooden docks, a day parking area, and the western trailhead for the park's hiking trail, which stretches 1.7 miles from Dunn Point to Rowell Cove.

Starting from Dunn Point, the hiking trail is wide and smooth, traveling through a forest that contains large white birch and northern cedar trees, as well as balsam fir, yellow birch, hemlock, and sugar maples. Along the trail old wooden signs identify some of these tree species.

The first part of the trail passes by a few campsites and travels along a section of park road to reenter the forest and trace the lakeshore to Rowell Cove, where there's another cluster of campsites, as well as a parking area and boat launch. A few side trails lead to viewpoints and swimming spots along the way. These side trails are marked on the park trail map and easy to identify because they are worn into the forest floor, but they aren't marked with signs.

As the trail nears its end, it becomes narrower and more rugged, with large exposed tree roots and rocky areas, as well as a couple of narrow bog bridges. The trail ends at a park road near the parking area for the Rowell Cove campsites.

On the edge of the North Maine Woods, the Moosehead Region has served as a special, seemingly remote spot for vacationers and outdoor enthusiasts since the mid-1800s.

A small island in Moosehead Lake is seen from one of the many viewpoints along the hiking trail in the park.

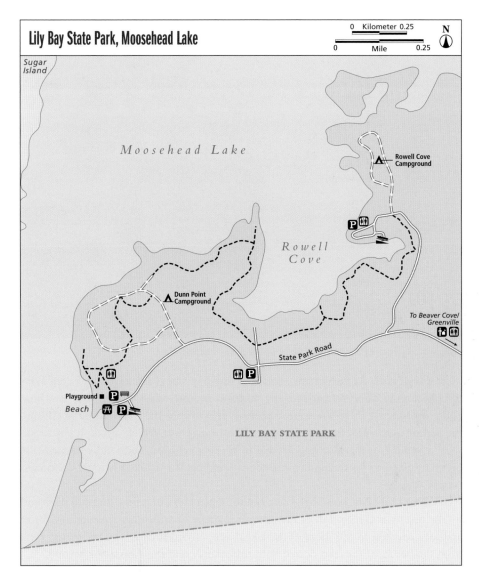

Lily Bay State Park, Moosehead Lake

0 Kilometer 0.25

0 Mile 0.25

N

Sugar Island

Moosehead Lake

Rowell Cove Campground

Rowell Cove

Dunn Point Campground

To Beaver Cove/ Greenville

State Park Road

Playground ■

Beach

LILY BAY STATE PARK

Formed by a glacier, Moosehead Lake covers an area of 117 square miles, according to the Lily Bay State Park brochure offered at the park entrance station. The lake is filled with togue, brook trout, and landlocked salmon.

In addition to the scenic Moosehead Lake, the area contains a number of impressive mountains that are popular for hiking, and it's a famous place for viewing some of Maine's most iconic wildlife: black bear, moose, and deer. Be careful while driving in the area, as moose-vehicle collisions are common, especially in May and June.

For more information: Visit www.maine.gov/lilybay or call the park at (207) 695-2700.

A moose chews aquatic plants in a pond in the Moosehead Region.

Personal note: At the entrance booth of Lily Bay State Park, a woman stepped out to collect admission—$4 each for my husband and me—and handed us a park brochure on May 14, 2016. We were exploring the park for the day, we told her. Using the park map in our brochure, she directed us to park our vehicle at Dunn Point. She then reminded us that our dog needed to be kept on leash, and kindly advised that he might want to go swimming at the boat landing. We thanked her and continued on our way.

I'd heard Lily Bay State Park was a beautiful place to camp, but I was still surprised by the quality and seclusion of the campsites, many of which are separated by forest and located close to the shore of the lake. I was also taken aback by the scenic view from the beach, of the lake, dotted with tiny islands, and the mountains beyond.

The park's trail—which is the epitome of family friendly—was infested with chattering red squirrels. I would have liked to watch their playful antics longer as they chased each other through the trees, leaping and climbing with remarkable ease, but that would have been torture for our dog Oreo, who has great anger for the little rodents, a condition that I hear is common among canines.

We had prepared to be assaulted by blackflies that day, but to our surprise, we didn't even need the insect repellent. Perhaps it was too early in the year for them. Or maybe the fresh breeze off the lake was enough to keep them at bay. Whatever the reason, we were happy to enjoy the warm, sunny day without being bitten by what's been referred to as "Maine's state bird" on many a T-shirt and bumper sticker.

A stand of white pines line a small beach at the park.

At a particularly beautiful viewpoint along the trail, we sat down on the damp earth and ate lunch while listening to a loon's eerie call. As usual, we let Oreo wade into the water for a bit, though it must have been quite cold so early in the year.

We almost went the entire hike without seeing another soul, but near the end of our walk, we came across a family of five from Ellsworth. Laura and Kevin DiDonato were exploring the park with their sons, Noah, 9, Owen, 6, and Caleb, 3. All three boys appeared to be in high spirits and told me they'd just seen two white-tailed deer. The DiDonato family was on a mission to fill their Maine State Parks Passport, which includes 48 state parks and historic sites.

At each location the DiDonatos visit, they locate the "passport station," where they find a special stamp to mark their passport, proving that they've visited. Lily Bay State Park was their 11th stamp on the passport.

The Maine State Passport Program, run by the Maine Bureau of Parks and Lands, includes small prizes for collecting different numbers of stamps, with the grand prize for 48 stamps being a season pass to Maine state parks and historic sites. For more information, visit www.maine.gov/dacf/parks/discover_history_explore_nature/activities/passport_program.shtml.

Hike 13: Ferry Beach State Park in Saco

About these trails: On the coast of southern Maine, Ferry Beach State Park is named after an old ferry crossing on the nearby Saco River, used by people traveling along the beaches of New England. The 117-acre park features a long sandy beach, a mixed forest, Long Pond, and a boardwalk through a tupelo swamp, a rare habitat in Maine. A simple network of easy trails connects these diverse features.

Difficulty: Easy. The forest trails of the park have been smoothed and surfaced with gravel and include a few wide wooden bridges and boardwalks.

Dogs: Permitted on park trails year-round if kept on a leash not exceeding 4 feet in length. Dogs are not permitted on the beach May 1 through September 30. Visitors are expected to pick up after their dogs and dispose of waste properly.

Cost: Admission is $5 for adult Maine residents, $7 for adult nonresidents, $2 for senior nonresidents, $1 for children 5–11 years old, and free for seniors (65+) and children younger than 5 years old.

Access: The gates of Ferry Beach State Park are open 9 a.m. to sunset daily from Memorial Day to September 30. During the off-season the park's gates are closed, but people are still welcome to use the trails and visit the beach. During that time visitors simply park outside the gate, well out of the way of traffic, and enter the park on foot.

Wheelchair accessibility: The smooth gravel-surfaced trails of the park are generally wheelchair accessible, with some barriers. People who use wheelchairs may require assistance in some areas, according to the state park website.

Hunting: Not permitted.

Restrooms: Restrooms are located by the parking lot and are open Memorial Day to September 30.

How to get there: The park's address is 95 Bayview Road in Saco. To get there from Interstate 95, take exit 36 to Interstate 195, then take exit 2A and turn right onto Main Street in Saco. Drive about 1 mile to a four-way intersection where you'll turn left onto Route 9 (Beach Street, which turns into Ferry Road). Continue on Route 9 for 2.7 miles, then turn left onto Bayview Road. Drive 0.3 mile and the park entrance will be on your right.

GPS coordinates: 43.481541', -70.392883'

Connecting all of the park's natural features is a network of easy forest trails that totals 1.3 miles of walking. There's the Tupelo Trail (0.4 mile), Red Oak Trail (0.2 mile), White Oak Trail (0.4 mile), Greenbriar Trail (0.1 mile), and Witchhazel Trail (0.1 mile). Also, a 0.1-mile path leads from the parking area to the beach, passing under Seaside Avenue along the way.

Interpretive signs located along the trails help visitors learn more about the history and wide variety of habitats found on the property. For example, at both ends of the boardwalk leading through the 100-acre tupelo swamp are displays explaining that black tupelo trees are rare at this latitude. The displays also offer a detailed

A loon in winter plumage swims in the ocean near the sandy Ferry Beach.

description of the trees so visitors can try to identify them as they walk along the boardwalk.

The park also features picnic tables and benches, restrooms, changing rooms, and a nature center providing guided nature programs.

While Ferry Beach sees most of its traffic during the summer, in the winter local residents often travel the park's trail network by cross-country skis and snowshoes, and the park's Long Pond is sometimes used for ice-skating.

Many people who visit the park just want to spend time on its beautiful sand beach. From the parking lot, an easy gravel footpath leads directly to the beach, passing through a habitat of sand dunes and pitch pines. These dunes provide an important barrier that prevents erosion along the beach and serves as a nesting area for many bird species. Visitors are asked to stay off this fragile environment.

For more information: Visit www.maine.gov/ferrybeach or call (207) 283-0067.

Personal note: It was during December when I drove to Boston to visit a longtime friend, and on my way I stopped in southern Maine for a short hike at Ferry Beach State Park. It was nice to break up the long drive with a walk through the woods and along the beach, which I hear can get crowded in the summer. But on that particular day, I saw only a few other visitors.

Walking on the boardwalk through the park's tupelo swamp, I tried my best to identify the rare black tupelo trees. It might have been easier if the trees hadn't already dropped their small oval leaves, but I'm almost positive I found them based on their deeply fissured bark and the branches growing perpendicular to their trunks. I'd like

A boardwalk travels through a tupelo swamp in the park.

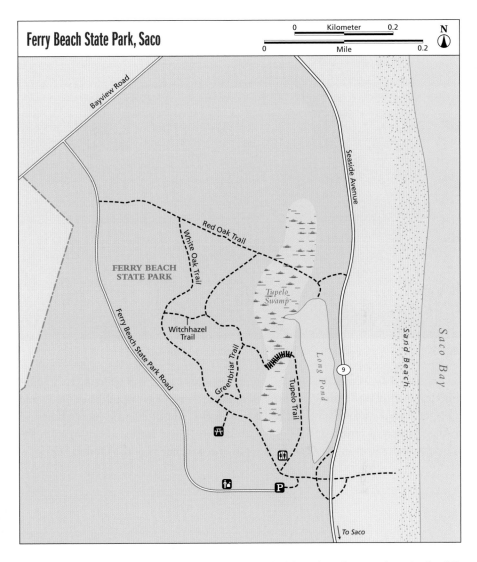

to return another season, when the trees are still holding their leaves. I hear in the fall, black tupelo leaves turn brilliant red.

Since I was traveling that weekend, I didn't have my dog Oreo with me on the hike, and that made it a lot easier to view wildlife. Flitting through the evergreen trees were little golden-crowned kinglets, tufted titmice, and black-capped chickadees. And while roaming the quiet sand beach, I stopped to photograph a common loon fishing offshore. In gray and white winter plumage, the loon took no notice of me as it wrestled with large fish for several minutes. I'm still not sure if the bird ever actually ate its catch.

Much farther out into the bay, a group of black scoters—a type of diving duck—bobbed on the waves. It was my first time seeing the species, and at the time, I didn't

A trail lined with a wooden fence leads to a big sand beach at the park.

know what they were. Later, by studying the photos I took and referring to a guide, I determined it was a group of black scoters; the male has a solid black body and a bright orange-yellow knob at the base of its bill, and the female has a distinctive feather pattern of brown and light grayish brown. These stocky ducks breed in the subarctic and winter offshore, along the east and west coasts of the United States.

Hike 14: Quoddy Head State Park in Lubec

About these trails: On the easternmost peninsula of the United States, Quoddy Head State Park features the historic red-and-white-striped West Quoddy Head Lighthouse, as well as about 5 miles of hiking trails that vary in difficulty and visit stunning outlooks along the rocky coastline. The 541-acre park, which is open for day use only, also features interpretive displays, a bog boardwalk, picnic areas, restrooms, and a cobblestone beach.

Difficulty: Easy to moderate, depending on the trails you explore in the park, which is home to about 5 miles of trails. The trails closest to the parking areas are wide and surfaced with gravel, making them smooth and easy to walk. Farther from the parking areas, the trails become narrow, hilly, and rough, with an abundance of exposed tree roots and rocks.

Dogs: Permitted if kept on a leash no longer than 4 feet at all times. Visitors are expected to pick up after their dogs and dispose of waste properly.

Cost: $3 for adult Maine residents, $4 for adult nonresidents, $1 for senior nonresidents, $1 for children 5–11 years old, and free for children under 5 and Maine seniors (65+).

Access: The park is open 9 a.m. to sunset daily from May 15 to October 15; visitors can continue to use the park during the off-season by parking outside the gate (which will be closed) and walking in during the same hours. Keep in mind that park facilities, such as outhouses, are closed during the off-season, and camping is prohibited in the park year-round. The lighthouse is home to a visitor center, open 10 a.m. to 4 p.m. from Memorial Day weekend through mid-October.

Wheelchair accessibility: Handicapped parking and a wheelchair-accessible outhouse are located by West Quoddy Head Lighthouse, and a wheelchair-accessible ramp leads up to the lighthouse. The visitor center is also wheelchair accessible.

Hunting: Permitted, but prohibited between June 1 and Labor Day. Also, hunting is prohibited within 1,000 feet of the lighthouse at all times, and the discharge of any weapon is prohibited from or within 300 feet of any picnic area, camping area or campsite, parking area, building, shelter, boat launch site, posted trail, or other developed area.

Restrooms: Outhouses are located at two out of the three parking areas.

How to get there: The park is located at the end of South Lubec Road in Lubec. To get there, start at the intersection of Route 1 and Route 189 in Whiting. Turn onto Route 189 and drive 9.8 miles to downtown Lubec. Turn right onto South Lubec Road and drive about 3 miles to enter the park (the park starts after Carrying Place Cove Road, which will be on your right). Continue on South Lubec Road 1.6 miles and you'll reach a fork in the road and a brown sign for Quoddy Head State Park. If you veer left, you'll find a parking area atop a hill near the West Quoddy Head Lighthouse. If you veer right, you'll find another parking lot at a picnic area by the water. These parking areas are close together, so if you're going for a hike, it really doesn't matter which one you use. Handicapped parking is located beside the lighthouse.

GPS coordinates: 44.816193', -66.952924'

The 2-mile Coastal Trail in the park includes several wooden staircases.

The park features five named trails.

The Coastal Trail is 2 miles long and travels over dramatic ocean cliffs from Quoddy Head Lighthouse to Carrying Place Cove, where it meets Thompson Trail. Beginning by the lighthouse, the Coastal Trail starts out as an easy walk along the coast on a wide path surfaced with gravel. Interpretive displays about the lighthouse and Maine whales are located along this portion of the trail, as well as several memorial benches where people can rest and take in the views.

The Coastal Trail becomes progressively difficult as it narrows and travels over the rugged landscape. Expect exposed tree roots, rocks, and steep staircases. The second half of the trail is not for young children, due to many dangerous cliffs. Along the way side trails spur off of this main trail to visit the landmarks Gulliver's Hole (a narrow chasm in the dark volcanic rock that forms the cliffs along the coast), High Ledge (a 150-foot-high bluff), and Green Point (a large ledge outcropping with spectacular views).

Thompson Trail is 1.25 miles and travels through the mixed forest from Carrying Place Cove to the Bog Trail. It's easy to moderate in difficulty, navigating a few hills and muddy areas. The trail is narrow in some places and wide in others, and it also includes a narrow bog bridge. This is a great trail to look for wildflowers and a variety of other forest plants.

The Bog Trail is a 1-mile round-trip and ends with a wide, wooden boardwalk that travels out into a coastal plateau bog with subarctic and arctic plants rarely seen south of Canada. The boardwalk forms a loop, and along the way are interpretive displays about how peatland is formed and the different plants found in the habitat.

The Inland Trail is 0.4 mile long and spans from the park's south parking area to the intersection with the Bog Trail and Thompson Trail. This is the most improved section of trail in the park. Wide and surfaced with gravel, this trail travels through a hilly conifer forest abundant in mosses and lichens. For families with young children, a hike combining this trail and the Bog Trail would be a great 1.8-mile adventure, out and back.

And finally, the Coast Guard Trail is a 1-mile horseshoe-shaped trail that begins and ends at different points near the lighthouse. The trail traces the rocky coast to visit an overlook of Lubec Channel.

Most visitors to the park are instantly drawn to the West Quoddy Head Lighthouse, which has served as a beacon for ships off the rocky coast of Maine for more than 200 years. The original lighthouse was commissioned by President Thomas Jefferson and built in 1808, according to information provided by the Maine Bureau of Parks and Lands. However, the present house is a bit younger, dating back to 1858. It

West Quoddy Head Lighthouse, which has served for a beacon for ships off the rocky coast of Maine for more than 200 years, stands on the easternmost peninsula of the United States in Quoddy Head State Park.

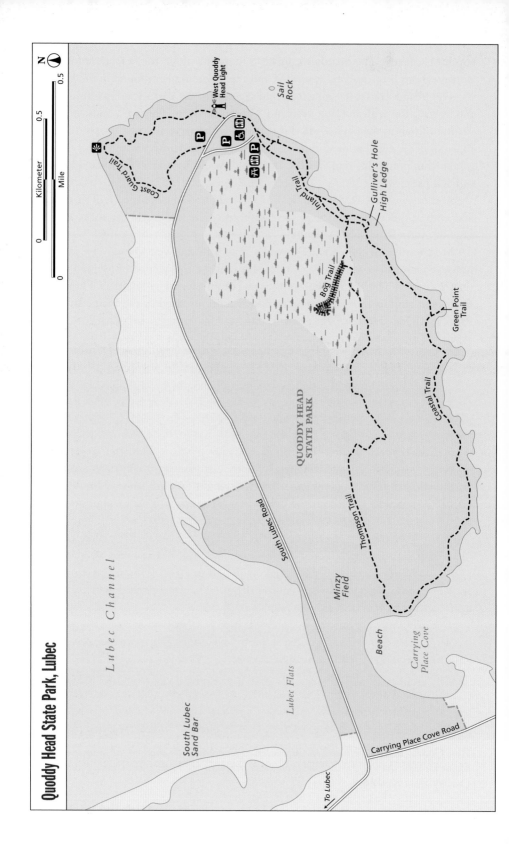

Quoddy Head State Park, Lubec

N

Kilometer
0   0.5

Mile
0   0.5

Lubec Channel

South Lubec Sand Bar

Lubec Flats

South Lubec Road

To Lubec

Carrying Place Cove Road

Beach

Carrying Place Cove

Minzy Field

Thompson Trail

QUODDY HEAD STATE PARK

Bog Trail

Coastal Trail

Green Point Trail

Gulliver's Hole
High Ledge

Inland Trail

Coast Guard Trail

West Quoddy Head Light

Sail Rock

Sheep laurel blossoms add color to the bog at Quoddy Head State Park in early June.

was staffed by lighthouse keepers until 1988, when the US Coast Guard automated the light.

Today, visitors can picnic on the lawn beside the lighthouse, where a stone monument marks the location as the "Easternmost Point in the USA." From that point you can look across Quoddy Channel to the cliffs of Grand Manan Island in New Brunswick, Canada. And closer, just offshore, is Sail Rock, which reportedly caused many shipwrecks in the past and belongs to the United States.

While exploring the park, keep an eye out for local wildlife. The tall ocean cliffs offer great vantage points for observing whales as well as sea ducks and other birds fishing offshore. During spring and fall migration, hundreds of shorebirds congregate near the park's western boundary at Lubec Flats and Carrying Place Outlet, according to the Maine Bureau of Parks and Lands.

For more information: Visit www.maine.gov/quoddyhead or call (207) 733-0911.

Personal note: When people learn that I write about hiking trails in Maine, they often ask me about my favorite trail. And while I find it impossible to select just one trail to be my favorite, it's easy for me to come up with a list of favorites—places that I find to be especially beautiful and interesting in Maine. Admittedly, it's a long list and only getting longer.

On June 2, 2016, Quoddy Head State Park became one of those favorite places for me. The views were spectacular, the habitats diverse, and the trails interesting and well maintained. The park offered so many opportunities to explore and learn about

The Coastal Trail in the park leads to numerous outlooks along the rocky coastline.

history, geology, and nature, and this experience was enhanced by the many interpretive displays located along the trails.

With my dog Oreo for company, I hiked four of the five trails in the park (we didn't make it to the Coast Guard Trail) for about 4.5 miles of walking.

The bright sun quickly warmed my skin, yet the temperature remained in the mid-60s. A cool, fresh breeze blew steadily from the ocean, banishing the blackflies and mosquitoes that so often accompany me during hikes that time of year. The conditions were ideal.

I especially enjoyed Green Point, which visitors had adorned with piles of carefully balanced rocks. Park managers often dislike visitors creating these rock piles (known as cairns) because they can confuse trail users and the movement of rocks can cause erosion. But in this case, I have to admit that the rock piles added a magical feeling to the location.

Hike 15: Hirundo Wildlife Refuge in Old Town

About these trails: Hirundo Wildlife Refuge, which celebrated its 50th anniversary in 2015, is a 2,460-acre preserve in Alton and Old Town that includes a vast network of trails, open to the public year-round, and sections of the Pushaw and Dead Streams, which can be explored by canoe and kayak.

Difficulty: Easy to moderate. Hirundo Wildlife Refuge is home to nearly 7 miles of trails that vary in difficulty. None of the trails climbs any steep slopes. The most difficult trails of the network have tricky footing due to exposed tree roots and rocks.

Dogs: Not permitted.

Cost: Free, though donations can left in locked boxes located at trailhead kiosks or by visiting www.hirundomaine.org/support.

Access: The trails are open dawn to dusk year-round. The refuge's main entrance, known as Gate 1, is open to vehicle traffic 9 a.m. to 6 p.m. April 15 to October 31, and 10 a.m. to 4 p.m. November 1 to January 31. If the many gates to the refuge are closed, there is plenty of room to park outside the gates and explore the trails from there. If visiting, sign a registry at Gates 1, 2, or 6. Smoking, fires, bicycles, and motor-driven vehicles are not permitted.

Wheelchair accessibility: While the trails and facilities of Hirundo may not meet ADA standards, there are several routes, trails, and scenic spots past Gate 1 that are wheelchair accessible, with the possibility of the wheelchair user needing some assistance. From the main parking area past Gate 1, the packed gravel road leading to the Parker Reed Shelter is smooth and may be wheelchair accessible, as is the connecting Pond Trail, which leads along the shore of Lac d'Or, where herons, ducks, frogs, turtles, and beavers are often seen. Hirundo is currently working with the University of Maine to construct a new 0.55-mile trail that meets ADA standards. This trail will travel through a field, along Lac d'Or, and into the forest to Pushaw Stream. And along the trail, Hirundo staff plan to plant a variety of native vegetation. Hirundo also just created a ramp to an outhouse near the Gate 1 parking area.

Hunting: Not permitted.

Restrooms: An outhouse is located at the main parking area by the Parker Reed Shelter, which is past Gate 1. A second outhouse is located just past Gate 6, with a third outhouse located at the intersection of Hemlock and Beech trails at the south end of the refuge.

How to get there: The physical address of the refuge is 1107 West Old Town Road in Old Town. Take Interstate 95 to exit 197 (Old Town/Hudson). At the end of the ramp, turn left onto Route 43 (Hudson Road) and drive west 4.75 miles. Look for large red signs on your right. Gate 1, the main gate, is marked by the first and largest of these signs. There are six other gates marked by red signs. In the winter an area in front of Gate 1 is plowed. Park outside Gate 1 but do not block the gate.

Gate 1 bars a road that leads to the northern half of the trail network. Gate 6, across the road, bars the Trapper's Trail, which leads into the southern half of the trail network.

GPS coordinates: 44.984658', -68.784493'

Named after the Latin word for "swallow," Hirundo was founded in 1965 by Oliver Larouche, who expanded his family's 3-acre camp to the present 2,460-acre refuge with an endowment from Parker Reed. Larouche's intent was for the land to be

A frog pops its head above the surface of Lac d'Or, a man-made pond in Hirundo Wildlife Refuge.

a "haven for wildlife." To improve wildlife diversity, he planted a variety of fruit-bearing trees and shrubs, lined the open fields on the property with tree swallow nest boxes, and erected wood duck nesting boxes along the banks of Pushaw Stream.

In 1983 Larouche and his wife, June, deeded the land to the University of Maine, and the couple funded research on fish, birds, and mammals on the property. The Larouche family continues to guide the Hirundo Board of Trustees, encouraging public access, outdoor education, and above all, the protection of wildlife and wildlife habitats.

Over the years, Hirundo has developed a reputation of being a family friendly location to learn about nature. With a wide variety of wildlife habitats, the refuge is an excellent place for viewing wildlife. The streams are home to beavers, river otters, muskrats, and snapping turtles, and the wetlands attract a wide variety of waterfowl and wading birds. The fields and nesting boxes attract songbirds, and the pond is alive with several species of frogs.

To help visitors learn and see more of the wildlife and plant life in the refuge, Hirundo naturalist Gudrun Keszöcze works with wildlife experts throughout Maine to organize nature and recreational programs at the refuge year-round, including guided nature walks and paddles, citizen science projects, and presentations held in the Parker Reed Shelter on nature-related topics.

The refuge has several entrances or gates and is bisected by Route 43.

The northern half of the refuge features a network of 3.2 miles of trails: the interpretive 0.4-mile Wabanaki Trail, which travels along the edge of Pushaw Stream; the 0.2-mile Big Spring Trail, which crosses a field and passes vernal pools and streams; the 0.3-mile Thorn Plum Trail, named for its thorn plum (hawthorn) trees; the 0.3-mile White Pine Trail; the 0.3-mile Conifer Trail; the 0.8-mile Pond Trail; and the 0.9-mile Pushaw Stream Trail.

Also on the north side of Route 43 is Parker Reed Shelter, where many of the refuge meetings and programs take place. The small red building is located near the shore of Lac d'Or, a 4-acre man-made pond that is home to frogs, dragonflies, and often mallards and other ducks.

The southern half of the trail network consists of about 3.5 miles of trails: the 1-mile Trapper's Trail, which is wide and ends at a small shelter; the 0.3-mile Vernal Pool Trail, which is short but difficult because of tricky footing; the 0.5-mile Indian Pipe Trail, for which there is an interpretive brochure; the 0.8-mile Hemlock Trail; and the 0.9-mile Beech Trail.

The Parker Reed Shelter, the hub of activity at Hirundo Wildlife Refuge, can be seen across Lac d'Or, a man-made pond built by the preserve's founder, Oliver Larouche.

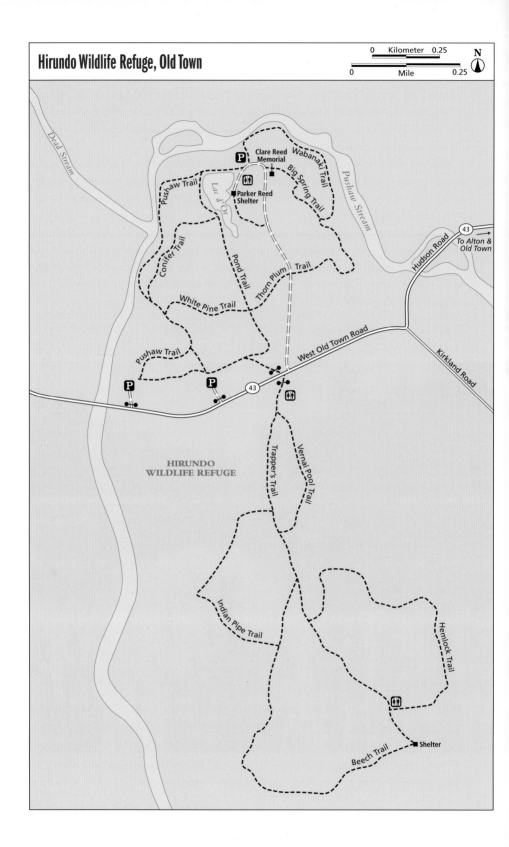

Hirundo Wildlife Refuge, Old Town

0   Kilometer   0.25
0   Mile   0.25

N

Dead Stream

Pushaw Trail

Clare Reed Memorial

Wabanaki Trail

Big Spring Trail

Pushaw Stream

Lac d'Or

Parker Reed Shelter

Conifer Trail

Pond Trail

Thorn Plum Trail

White Pine Trail

Pushaw Trail

West Old Town Road

Hudson Road

43

To Alton & Old Town

Kirkland Road

HIRUNDO WILDLIFE REFUGE

Trapper's Trail

Vernal Pool Trail

Indian Pipe Trail

Hemlock Trail

Beech Trail

Shelter

A sign marks an archaeological dig site at Hirundo Wildlife Refuge where artifacts from a Native American settlement were once found.

Paddling is another popular way to explore Hirundo. During the warm months the refuge offers the free use of canoes Wednesday through Sunday, weather dependent. However, visitors must reserve canoes in advance.

For more information: Visit www.hirundomaine.org or call the refuge at (207) 394-2171 and leave a message. The refuge naturalist will return your call within 24 hours. To reserve Hirundo canoes, call Hirundo caretaker Alivia Moore at (207) 745-6644 at least one day in advance.

Personal note: The end of winter was nowhere in sight on March 20, 2015, when Derek (my fiancé at the time, and now my husband) and I headed to Hirundo Wildlife Refuge with our cross-country skis. Tiny snowflakes sparkled in the muted sunlight as they fluttered to the ground, filling up the ski tracks that led into the woods beyond Gate 6.

I had visited Hirundo several times before to walk the trails, and I'd attended some of Hirundo's public nature programs, including a class on how to monitor the state's nine species of frogs. But it was my first time skiing on the property.

A short way down Trapper's Trail, we found a kiosk with a soggy registration sheet, a laminated trail map, and a locked donations box. Tucked in the woods nearby was an outhouse, complete with a crescent moon carved into the door.

The winter had been particularly stormy, but I didn't realize just how deep the snow cover was until I took off my skis to walk off-trail to photograph a pileated woodpecker. Without my skis keeping me afloat, I sank into the snow past my knees.

After wading a few steps, I abandoned my plan and struggled back into my skis, contenting myself in simply listening to the large bird's distinctive piping call as we skied along.

We skied down Trapper's Trail, which is wide, straight, and acts as a connector for all of the other trails on the southern portion of Hirundo. Along the way we passed side trails—Vernal Pool, Beech, Indian Pipe, and Hemlock trails—and at the far end of Trapper's Trail, a small wooden building welcomed us. We opened the door of the shelter to find a long wooden bench inside, and while we didn't have any use for it that day, I imagined in a few months it would be a good place to escape the bugs.

On our return to the trailhead, we explored Beech Trail, which wove through a large stand of beech trees, many still holding onto their crispy yellow leaves. Once again, we were startled by the call of a pileated woodpecker and the quick drumroll of it drilling on a nearby tree.

Upon returning to Route 43, I persuaded Derek to cross the road and join me on a short ski to the Parker Reed Shelter and frozen Lac d'Or in the northern portion of Hirundo. From there we wandered just a bit farther north, following the red blazes of the Wabanaki Trail to the edge of Pushaw Stream, where I spotted a white-tailed deer wading in the shallows. Excited that I might capture a great wildlife photo, I rushed forward with camera in hand, then suddenly realized that I was going to ski right off the snowy bank and into the water. I managed to stop myself by sitting down in the snow, relinquishing any hope of getting a good photo. The deer had dashed into the forest and out of sight before I recovered my dignity.

Hike 16: Hundred Acre Wood in Brooklin

About this trail: A 113-acre preserve in the small coastal town of Brooklin, Hundred Acre Wood was donated to the Blue Hill Heritage Trust in 2012 by Stephen Winthrop and his wife, M. Jane Williamson. The couple and their two daughters wished "to conserve its natural character and share a place to walk in the woods." They named the preserve and its 1.7-mile trail after the Hundred Acre Wood that is the setting of *Winnie-the-Pooh*, a 1926 book of children's stories by English author A. A. Milne that has since been resurrected in many books and animated cartoons.

Difficulty: Easy to moderate. The 1.7-mile Hundred Acre Wood Trail is well maintained and marked. The trail changes in elevation slightly and includes a few challenges, including rocky areas, exposed roots, and bog bridges.
Dogs: Permitted but must be kept on leash at all times. Carry out all pet waste.
Cost: Free. Donations can be made to Blue Hill Heritage Trust at www.bluehillheritagetrust.org.
Access: The preserve is open to the public during daylight hours year-round. The trails are for foot traffic only. Camping and fires are not permitted unless explicitly authorized by the Blue Hill Heritage Trust.

Wheelchair accessibility: The trail is not built to be wheelchair accessible. It is narrow and filled with rocks and tree roots.
Hunting: By permission only.
Restrooms: None.
How to get there: From the town of Blue Hill, drive south on Route 15-Route 176. Across from Beech Hill Road, turn left onto South Street-Route 175-Route 172. Drive 6 miles. Turn left onto Hales Hill Road. Drive 0.7 mile to a four-way intersection. Drive straight through the intersection onto High Street. About 500 feet from the intersection, the parking area to Hundred Acre Wood will be on the left.
GPS coordinates: 44.315997', -68.585325'

Winnie-the-Pooh's Hundred Acre Wood is a magical place, home to a forlorn donkey, bashful piglet, and friendly tiger. You won't find any of these fantastical creatures in Brooklin's Hundred Acre Wood, but you may stumble across Maine wildlife such as snowshoe hares, porcupines, squirrels, white-tailed deer, and a variety of songbirds as you explore the property's forests, wild blueberry patches, and small wetland areas.

A 1.7-mile loop trail, marked with blue blazes, travels close to the edges of the property and passes through a wide variety of habitats. The trail was constructed in 2013 with the help of consultant Cathy Rees, trail manager Ken Burgess, the Blue Hill Heritage Trust's volunteer crew, and the Brooklin Youth Corps.

"I would classify the trail as easy to moderate," said Burgess in a 2013 interview. "The inclines are gradual, and there are seventeen 8-foot bog bridges to traverse the areas that are sometimes wet."

The trail map available on the BHHT website includes two natural highlights: a white cedar forest and a glacial erratic, which is a rock that was moved from another location by glacial ice and deposited on the property thousands of years ago.

A trail travels through a mixed forest in the Hundred Acre Wood.

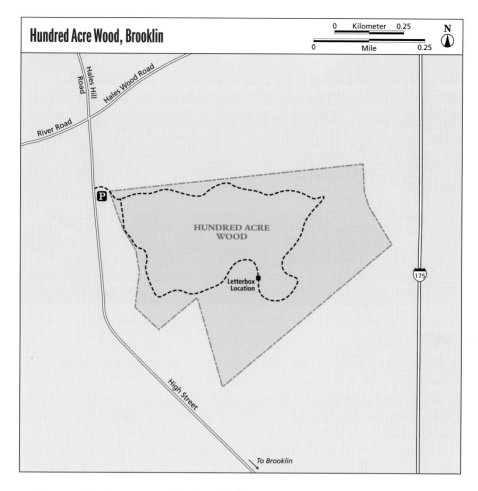

Interpretive signs created by Blue Hill Heritage Trust were installed along the trail with the help of students from Brooklin Elementary School. These signs offer information about different species of plants found along the trail, as well as local wildlife.

The trail also features a letterbox, a wooden container that is a part of an outdoor game that combines navigational skills and rubber stamp artistry. To learn more about letterboxing, check out www.letterboxing.org.

BHHT has erected letterboxes on all of its public trails, which are located in small preserves scattered throughout the towns of Blue Hill, Brooklin, Brooksville, Castine, Penobscot, Sedgwick, and Surry. A nonprofit organization, BHHT was founded in 1985 and by summer of 2016 had conserved more than 7,000 acres on the Blue Hill Peninsula. Some of the preserves feature trails, while others do not.

For more information: Call (207) 374-5118, visit www.bluehillheritagetrust.org, or e-mail info@bluehillheritagetrust.org. The land trust office is usually open 8:30 a.m. to 5 p.m. Monday through Friday, and is located in the William Carleton House

Rock piles called cairns help hikers stay on trail while crossing through a clearing in the Hundred Acre Wood.

at 258 Mountain Road in Blue Hill. However, the office may unexpectedly close when BHHT staff are out working on land trust property.

Personal note: Hundred Acre Wood is where I first saw a porcupine in the wild. Unfortunately, my dog Oreo was with me, so the event was more disruptive than I would have liked. But let's rewind for a moment.

It was mid-September in 2013 when the Hundred Acre Wood loop trail officially opened to the public, and I was eager to check it out. So with Oreo for company, I walked the new trail on that opening day.

My overall impression of the preserve was that it seemed a lot bigger than 113 acres, probably because of the many changes in landscape as we walked along the trail. One moment we were walking through a cedar stand, and the next, we were in a sea of ferns; then we were following cairns over exposed bedrock, surrounded by colorful lichens and low-bush blueberries.

We were about halfway through our walk when I spied the porcupine. The dark, spiky critter was slowly scaling a tree beside the trail, and Oreo seemed to have spotted it about the same time I did. Registering that it was a wild animal, Oreo started to whimper and yank on his leash, then started barking. It's funny how some animals, such as squirrels, get him riled up, while other animals, such as songbirds, don't bother him.

I normally would have sat quietly and watched the porcupine as it munched on tree bark, just to observe its behavior and take photos, but in this case I knew that remaining would only cause the wild animal (and Oreo) unnecessary stress. So after taking a couple quick photos of the porcupine, I continued along the trail, leaving the creature in peace.

Hike 17: Curtis Farm Preserve in Harpswell

About these trails: Curtis Farm Preserve, named after the last family to farm the property in 1940, is owned and maintained by the Harpswell Heritage Land Trust, which purchased the bulk of the property in 2011 with donations from more than 160 contributors. An additional 14 acres was added in 2013, bringing the preserve to 86 acres in total size—a large piece of land for the coastal town of Harpswell. The trail network within covers 1.25 miles and travels over mowed grass, forest floor, and narrow bog bridges.

Difficulty: Easy to moderate. Hiking from the shore to the field, you'll climb a considerable hill. The easiest part of the trail network is the wide trail that travels around the perimeter of Williams Field.

Dogs: Permitted but must be on leash during bird nesting season: April 15 to July 31. Dogs must be under voice control the rest of the year. Carry out all pet waste.

Cost: Free, though donations can be made to the Harpswell Heritage Land Trust at www .hhltmaine.org/donate.

Access: The trails are open year-round, and the parking lot is plowed during the winter. The trails are for foot traffic only; this includes snowshoeing and cross-country skiing. Open fires, camping, biking, and power-driven mobility devices are not permitted.

Wheelchair accessibility: The trails of Curtis Farm Preserve were not constructed to be wheelchair accessible.

Hunting: Permitted.

Restrooms: None.

How to get there: There are two parking areas for the preserve. From the intersection of Route 123 and Bath Road at Bowdoin College in Brunswick, follow Route 123 south for 11.4 miles, and the first preserve parking lot is on the right, on the edge of Williams Field. (Note: You'll pass Harpswell Neck Fire Department on the right soon before reaching the parking area.) To reach the second parking area, which is across from Basin Cove, continue on Route 123 south another 0.2 mile and turn right onto Ash Point Road; take your first right onto Basin Point Road and drive 0.5 mile to the parking lot on the right.

GPS coordinates: 43.761615', -70.013667'

Reed Coles, executive director of the Harpswell Heritage Land Trust, had this to say about Curtis Farm Preserve in a 2015 interview: "It is remarkable for the variety of habitats within just 86 acres, ranging from open old agricultural field . . . to mature oak forest, mature spruce fir forest, early successional shrubbery forest, to freshwater wetlands of two types, plus a pond, plus extensive coastal flats, mud flats that are of very high value both for shellfish and as wading bird habitat."

Harpswell Heritage Land Trust has conserved more than 1,400 acres in Harpswell. Of that land, 355 acres is owned by the land trust, and the rest is conserved by conservation easements on privately owned land. Overall, the land trust maintains about 7 miles of trails, split among several properties.

A sign marks a parking area for the preserve. Beyond it are bird nesting boxes scattered throughout Williams Field.

Curtis Farm Preserve's 1.25-mile trail network officially opened in June 2015. The trails are marked with blue and yellow painted blazes, and signs are located at each section. One trail travels around the perimeter of the 6-acre Williams Field, where nesting boxes and a variety of plants attract songbirds.

"This field, in the early part of the 20th century, was used for baseball games," said Coles. "Teams on Sundays would row over from Orrs Island and Bailey Island across Harpswell Sound and play the Harpswell Neck teams. Then from the '60s through the mid-'80s, the Boy Scouts and fire department had bean hole suppers here. They mowed the field, and put tables out, and put beans in a hole up behind these sumacs."

"It has essentially been a spot for community activity for 100-plus years now, and we hope that with these trails, it will continue to be an attractive spot for people to use," he added.

At the south edge of the field, a short side trail leads to a glacial erratic (a boulder left by a receding glacier) that is called "The Pebble." And at the north edge of the field, the Coves Trail enters the forest to travel to Curtis Cove and the parking area at Basin Cove. Along the way there is a partial outlook of Middle Bay. On a clear day visitors can see all the way to the White Mountains in New Hampshire from that spot. From there the trail descends through mature spruce-fir forest to reach the shore. Several bog bridges in this section of trail make the walk more interesting (and less muddy).

For more information: Visit the Harpswell Heritage Land Trust website at www .hhltmaine.org or call the land trust at (207) 721-1121.

Caterpillars munch on foliage on the outskirts of Williams Field in the preserve.

Personal note: Serenaded by crickets, I followed the trail along the edge of Williams Field and entered a stand of towering oak trees on a beautiful June afternoon, one day before the trails' grand opening. From the bushes nearby came the

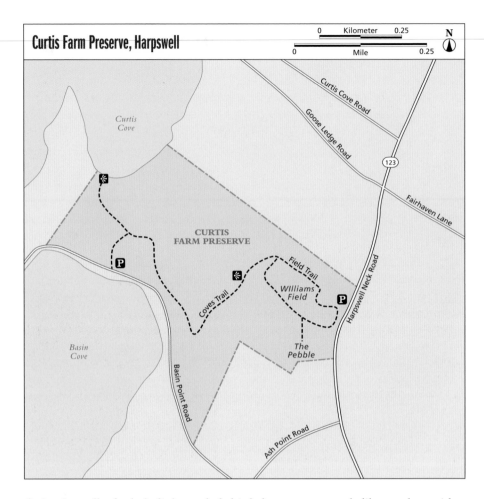

Curtis Cove Road

Goose Ledge Road

Curtis
Cove

123

Fairhaven Lane

CURTIS
FARM PRESERVE

P

Field Trail

Williams
Field

P

Coves Trail

Harpswell Neck Road

Basin
Cove

The
Pebble

Basin Point Road

Ash Point Road

distinctive call of a bobolink—a dark bird that to me sounds like a robot with a talent for melody.

Heading deeper into the woods on the Coves Trail, I was accompanied by a group of noisy waxwings, moving from the top of one birch tree to the next. Then three wild turkeys crossed the trail ahead of me and disappeared into the underbrush. And on the shore of Curtis Cove, I spotted two mallard ducks, a male and female swimming through the seaweed.

As I moseyed back to the trailhead, I took the time to enjoy the many spring blossoms, from pink lady's slipper orchids sprouting from the mossy forest floor to common bluets dotting the edge of the field. In Maine, spring is an excellent time to find wildflowers of all kinds, especially in the forest.

Though coastal Maine is now an easy place to pick up harmful ticks, I managed to get through the walk tick free. I did, however, pick up a tiny green inchworm, which I carefully plucked off my shoulder and placed on a tree before leaving the preserve.

Hike 18: Northeast Penjajawoc Preserve in Bangor

About these trails: Comprising 80.5 acres of forestland and wetlands in Bangor, the Northeast Penjajawoc Preserve is owned and maintained by the Bangor Land Trust for wildlife and low-impact public recreation. On the property about 2 miles of trails form the rough shape of a figure eight, leading visitors through a variety of habitats.

Difficulty: Easy to moderate. The preserve trails form a figure eight shape, of sorts. Each loop is about 1 mile long. The trails travel over what is known as "unimproved forest floor," which means the ground has not been smoothed out or surfaced with gravel. In some places the forest floor is quite smooth and covered with soft pine needles, whereas other sections of trail are very rocky. While there is no significant change in elevation, the trails do travel over a few small hills. Also, pay attention to your feet as you walk along long stretches of narrow bog bridges.

Dogs: Permitted if kept on leash at all times. Visitors are expected to pick up after their dogs and dispose of waste properly.

Cost: Free.

Access: Open year-round. The trails are for hiking and mountain biking, and in the winter, snowshoeing.

Wheelchair accessibility: The trails were not constructed to be wheelchair accessible. They are rocky in many places and include narrow bog bridges.

Hunting: Permitted, in accordance with Maine hunting laws and seasons.

Restrooms: None.

How to get there: Take Interstate 95 to exit 186 and turn right onto Stillwater Avenue. Drive 1.1 miles (straight through the traffic light at the Stillwater Avenue–Hogan Road intersection) and turn left onto Kittredge Road. Drive 0.1 mile and turn right at the stop sign to remain on Kittredge Road. Continue another 0.8 mile to the preserve trailhead, which will be on your left, just before the pavement ends. (The kiosk is set back into the woods a bit.) Park at the side of the road, well out of the way of traffic.

GPS coordinates: 44.853383', -68.743426'

A self-guided nature tour, which involves a brochure that corresponds with six numbered signs or "nature stations" along the trail, can help visitors better interpret their surroundings. This brochure is sometimes available at the trailhead kiosk, but it's also available on the Bangor Land Trust website, www.bangorlandtrust.org.

The six habitats outlined by the nature tour are: (1) an upland forest dominated by red oak, white pine, red maple, and balsam fir trees; (2) a cattail marsh; (3) a shady riparian forest that borders a small stream flowing into Penjajawoc Marsh; (4) an early successional forest composed mostly of deciduous trees such as quaking and big tooth aspen, gray and paper birch, and red maple; (5) a vernal pool, a shallow depression in the forest floor that contains water for only part of the year; and (6) a mixed graminoid-shrub marsh.

Visitors enter the preserve on one trail, which starts right by the trailhead kiosk on Kittredge Road. Marked with small Bangor Land Trust signs, the trail immediately

Sunlight filters through a fern in the preserve.

A bog bridge helps hikers keep their feet dry beside a cattail marsh in the preserve.

enters a beautiful stand of tall white pine trees. The forest then changes to include a greater variety of trees, and the trail meets the first intersection in the preserve.

This intersection is the start of the main loop in the preserve, which is a little less than 1 mile long and includes the nature stations 1 and 2 along its north side (the trail on the right as you're approaching the intersection.) The loop also includes several wooden bridges and steps, which are a bit tricky to navigate by mountain bike but can be fun for experienced cyclists.

At the far end of the first loop, a scenic wooden bridge crosses a stream that flows into Penjajawoc Marsh. On the bridge is nature station 3, and after crossing that bridge, you'll come to another trail intersection, which is the start to the second loop in the preserve. On the second loop you'll find stations 4, 5, and 6. The far end of the loop travels along the old Veazie Railroad bed—which acts as a connector trail to the Rolland F. Perry City Forest (also known as the Bangor City Forest) and Bangor Land Trust's North Penjajawoc Preserve and Walden-Parke Preserve.

Also of note: On the north side of the second loop is a side trail that leads to power lines and an overlook of a marsh. Keep in mind that, though the trail appears to continue across the power lines, beyond the power lines is private property.

The Northeast Penjajawoc Preserve was purchased by the Bangor Land Trust in 2007, with support from the Land for Maine's Future program and the North American Wetlands Conservation Fund. A nonprofit organization, the Bangor Land Trust was founded in 2001 and has since conserved more than 800 acres of land with public access in the Bangor area. In addition to the annual Pedal the Penobscot road

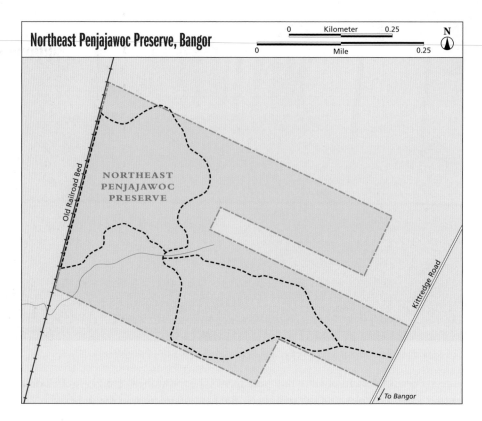

ride, Bangor Land Trust hosts monthly community events on its preserves, including nature walks and talks designed to engage people of all ages.

For more information: Visit www.bangorlandtrust.org, where you'll find a trail map and brochure for the self-guided nature tour, as well as a calendar of public events hosted by the land trust. You can also visit the BLT office at 8 Harlow Street in Bangor, call (207) 942-1010, or e-mail info@bangorlandtrust.org.

Personal note: After a long weekend of wedding festivities for my friends Kim and Chris in Bucksport, I was pretty much a zombie on Sunday, August 7, 2016, when I decided to get some fresh air at the Northeast Penjajawoc Preserve with my husband Derek and our dog Oreo. Right off the bat, we came across Lucy Quimby, president of the Bangor Land Trust, walking the preserve trails with a hiking companion. She thanked us for having Oreo on leash (which is a rule in the preserve) and told us that she'd just come across some hikers who had their dog off leash. Nevertheless, she had tried to help the people, who had become lost in the trail network. They were looking for the Veazie Railroad bed, and she pointed them in the right direction.

That day, the preserve trails were well maintained and they seemed to be well traveled, with bike tire tracks imprinted into the few muddy spots, along with boot prints.

In an area of the preserve where the songbirds were especially noisy, I took the time to pause and photograph a female black-and-white warbler as it hopped around

The trails in the preserve travel through a beautiful mixed forest.

on a fallen tree. And I unsuccessfully chased after a tiny wood frog hopping through the leaf litter. Derek and Oreo had walked on ahead of me, as they often do.

By the time we returned to the trailhead, we had a few itchy mosquito bites but we felt less like zombies, having benefited, no doubt, from a bit of exercise and fresh air.

The forest was a great place to identify a variety of trees, and I imagine it's quite beautiful in the autumn, with all the maples, birches, oaks, and aspens in full color.

Hike 19: Holbrook Island Sanctuary State Park in Brooksville

About these trails: Located in the coastal town of Brooksville, Holbrook Island Sanctuary State Park was donated to the state of Maine in 1971 by a local resident, Anita Harris. A nature lover, Harris wished this gift would "preserve for the future a piece of unspoiled Maine that [she] used to know." Within the park are nine trails that together make up nearly 11 miles of hiking.

Difficulty: Easy to moderate, depending on the trails you choose to hike within the park. Some trails are easy and travel over smooth terrain, such as the 0.7-mile Backshore Trail, while others are more challenging, such as the steep 0.9-mile Summit Trail.

Dogs: Permitted if kept on a leash no longer than 4 feet at all times. Violators of this rule will be asked to leave the park. Carry out all pet waste.

Cost: Free.

Access: The park is open to the public year-round, 9 a.m. to sunset, for hiking, snowshoeing, and cross-country skiing, though trails are not groomed. Camping is not permitted, and fires are permitted in park grills only.

Wheelchair accessibility: Trails, picnic tables, and parking areas are "somewhat accessible," according to the Maine Bureau of Parks and Lands. However, the trails in the park were not constructed to be wheelchair accessible and they do not meet ADA standards. Some trails are smoother and wider than others in the

park. For example, the Backshore Trail travels over a mowed grass surface and is fairly wide.

Hunting: Not permitted.

Restrooms: One restroom is located at park headquarters on Indian Bar Road, and another restroom is located at the dock across from Holbrook Island off Back Road. Both are marked on the park trail map.

How to get there: The park is accessed off Cape Rosier Road in Brooksville. From the intersection of Route 175 and Route 15 in Brooksville, take Route 175 north 0.6 mile, then continue straight onto Route 176 (Coastal Road). Drive 4.4 miles, then turn left onto Cape Rosier Road. Drive 1.6 miles and Back Road will be on your right; Back Road leads into the park to several trailheads in the sanctuary. Or you can continue on Cape Rosier Road another mile to Otis Gray Road (on your right), at the end of which is the parking area for Fresh Pond Trail.

GPS coordinates: Fresh Pond Nature Trailhead: 44.342947', -68.785377'

The park is 1,230 acres and protects a variety of habitats, including old fields, a pond, an estuary, a saltwater marsh, the mossy evergreen forests of Bakeman Mountain, a beaver flowage, and rocky beaches on Penobscot Bay. It also includes Holbrook Island, a small isle off the coast near Goose Falls.

The park also features a number of old family cemeteries, old foundations, and impressive stone walls that remain from people who used to live and farm on the land—the Bakemans, Hutchinses, Howards, and Grays.

Seaweed clings to a barnacle-encrusted rock on a rocky beach accessible by the Backshore Trail of the park.

A part of Maine's state park system, the park is managed in a way that keeps with Anita Harris's vision. Therefore, the park has not and will not be altered by modern park facilities and management techniques. A network of old farm roads and paths have simply been turned into blazed hiking trails for visitors to explore, and the forest and other natural habitats have been left in Mother Nature's hands.

The park features about 11 miles of easy-to-moderate hikes, with trails varying in length from 0.6 mile to 2 miles. Some trails are connected, while others stand on their own. Some trails form a loop hike, while others must be hiked out and back.

In all, there are nine trails: Bakeman Farm Trail, Fresh Pond Trail, Aaron Trail, Summit Trail, Mountain Loop, Beaver Flowage Trail, Goose Falls Trail, Backshore Trail, and Iceworks Trail.

A favorite among families is the 1.4-mile Fresh Pond Trail, which is an interpretive loop trail with 24 numbered signs. At each sign hikers can stop and read about a natural feature of their surroundings from a brochure, which is available at the trailhead kiosk. Features covered in the brochure include native plants, such as bunchberry, fragrant water-lily, and northern white cedar, and wildlife typically seen around Fresh Pond, such as wood ducks.

While the parking area for Fresh Pond Trail is at the end of Otis Gray Road, the trail actually starts about halfway down the road, at the edge of a lawn near two picnic tables. Signs mark the trailhead and the parking area. The trail starts out as easy, smooth and wide, then becomes more challenging as it splits and travels around Fresh

Fresh Pond Trail leads to wetlands and a body of water called Fresh Pond in the park.

Pond to form a loop. At the far end of the pond, the trail is narrow and travels over some rougher terrain, with exposed tree roots and rocks.

For people looking for a shorter, easier walk, the 0.6-mile Backshore Trail is a wide, smooth path that starts at Indian Bar Road (off Back Road) and leads through old farmland to a beautiful, rocky beach. Along the way you'll pass by some old foundations, an old root cellar, and the old Bakeman-Hutchins family cemetery.

And for people looking for more of a challenge, the Mountain Loop and Summit Trail on Bakeman Mountain (also known as Backwoods Mountain) are both narrow, rocky, and crisscrossed with exposed tree roots. These trails travel through a mossy, whimsical forest to a nice, partial view of the ocean from the north slope of the mountain.

The park is a spectacular place for bird-watchers. At several of the trailheads is a bird checklist for the park, which includes more than 200 species of birds, as well as their seasonal occurrence and relative abundance on the property. Species found on the property include the common loon, great blue heron, American black duck, red-breasted merganser, bald eagle, ruffed grouse, killdeer, great black-backed gull, belted kingfisher, northern flicker, gold-crowned kinglet, cedar waxwing, dark-eyed junco, and many more.

For young hikers planning to make multiple trips to the park (with an adult hiking partner), the nonprofit Friends of Holbrook Island Sanctuary has created the "I Hiked Holbrook" trail challenge, a scavenger hunt to find posted symbols on each of the nine trails. After finding each symbol, participants must draw it on their challenge

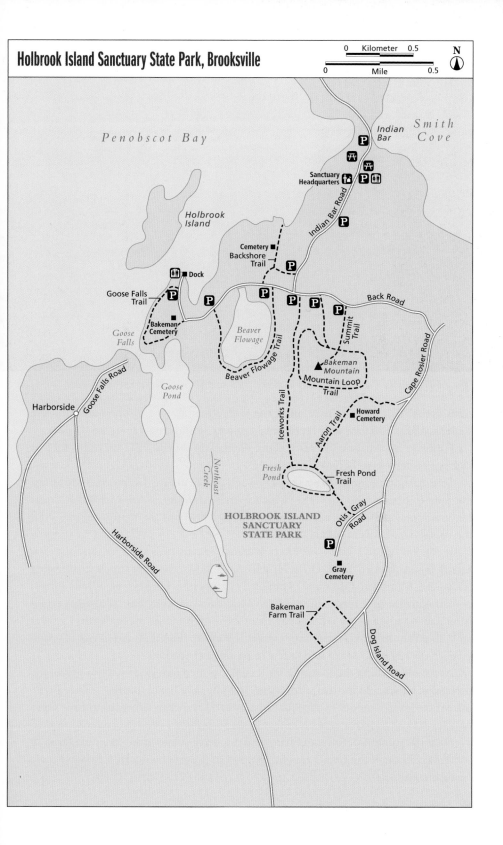

Holbrook Island Sanctuary State Park, Brooksville

0   Kilometer   0.5

0   Mile   0.5

N

Smith Cove

Penobscot Bay

Indian Bar

Sanctuary Headquarters

Holbrook Island

Indian Bar Road

Cemetery Backshore Trail

Dock

Goose Falls Trail

Back Road

Goose Falls

Bakeman Cemetery

Beaver Flowage

Summit Trail

Cape Rosier Road

Beaver Flowage Trail

▲ *Bakeman Mountain*

Mountain Loop Trail

Goose Pond

Iceworks Trail

Harborside

Goose Falls Road

Aaron Trail

Howard Cemetery

Northeast Creek

Fresh Pond

Fresh Pond Trail

Otis Gray Road

HOLBROOK ISLAND SANCTUARY STATE PARK

Harborside Road

Gray Cemetery

Bakeman Farm Trail

Dog Island Road

The park's Summit Trail leads through a mossy forest to the top of Backwoods Mountain.

cards, along with the date they hiked the trail. When all nine symbols are gathered, students grades K–8 can turn their cards into park headquarters for a free T-shirt.

For more information: To learn about the park in general, call (207) 326-4012 or visit www.maine.gov/holbrookisland.

Personal note: A warm front swept through Maine in early February 2016, bringing temperatures in the low 50s—which is really unheard of for a state that boasts long snowy winters. But I wasn't about to complain about the unusual respite from the cold. Instead, I went hiking in a T-shirt.

It was my second visit to Holbrook Island Sanctuary State Park, and my dog Oreo's first. I decided we'd start with what looked like the park's most challenging trails—the Mountain Loop and Summit Trail, because I always enjoy climbing a good mountain. As it turns out, Bakeman Mountain (which is also called Backwoods Mountain on some maps) is home to one of the most beautiful mossy forests I've ever seen, abundant in white cedar and fragrant balsam fir. The trail started out easy and gradual, then became rocky with a few steep, slippery sections.

As we hiked along the foot of a small cliff, I spotted two giant piles of porcupine droppings, which told me that a porcupine must be denning up nearby—likely in the many nooks and crannies of the cliff. Seeing that, I was especially glad to have Oreo on a leash.

Near the summit of the mountain, we ate a snack while sitting on a bench at an overlook. Through the trees I caught glimpses of the nearby ocean, where we were headed next.

The Backshore Trail was a completely different experience, traveling a mowed path through overgrown fields and past the remains of an old farm. Each stone wall and old foundation echoed stories of the past.

The trail ended at a rocky beach covered with seaweed, mussel shells, periwinkles, and barnacle-encrusted rocks. As usual, Oreo went straight to the water, and though technically it was the middle of winter, I allowed him to wade into the salty, frigid water and clamber over mounds of seaweed for a few minutes before reining him back in. The sun, dim in the overcast sky, was just touching the treetops when we left the beach to return to the car.

Hike 20: Fields Pond Audubon Center in Holden

About these trails: Fields Pond Audubon Center is one of eight wildlife sanctuaries owned and maintained by Maine Audubon, a nonprofit organization that works to conserve wildlife and wildlife habitats throughout the state by engaging people of all ages in education, conservation, and outdoor activities. There are about 5 miles of intersecting trails on the property, and these trails vary greatly in the habitats they travel through.

Difficulty: Easy to moderate. The easiest trails are near the Nature Center, traveling through nearby fields on mowed grass. Farther out, the forest trails are a bit more challenging, traveling over hills and tangles of exposed tree roots.

Dogs: Not permitted.

Cost: Free, but donations can be made in a donation box outside the Nature Center by the butterfly garden, as well as a donation box in the lobby of the Nature Center. Or you can donate online at www.maineaudubon.org, where you can also learn about becoming a Maine Audubon member.

Access: The trails are open year-round, dawn until dusk. The Nature Center is open 10 a.m. to 4 p.m. Thursday through Saturday and is closed Sunday. The Nature Center is open for groups by appointment Monday through Wednesday. In the winter the parking area is plowed and there is a groomed trail maintained by the Eastern Maine Snowmobilers that travels through the property to Fields Pond, a popular spot for ice-fishing.

Wheelchair accessibility: The Nature Center and the restrooms inside are wheelchair accessible. None of the trails meets ADA standards, but some of the trails near the Nature Center are wide and smooth, making them likely suitable for most wheelchairs. For example, a 0.25-mile gravel path that leads from the Nature Center through a meadow to the forest may be accessible to wheelchairs, and the mowed paths around the fields are free of tree roots and other barriers, making them great options for people with limited mobility. Fields Pond Audubon Center is currently working on building ADA-compliant trails and ramps to a frog pond on the property.

Hunting: Not permitted.

Restrooms: Located in the Nature Center, which is open 10 a.m. to 4 p.m. Thursday through Saturday.

How to get there: From Route 1A in Holden, turn onto Copeland Hill Road. If driving east toward Ellsworth, the turn will be on your right near the Myerowitz Chiropractic & Acupuncture Clinic, which has a yin-yang on its sign. Drive until you reach a stop sign. Turn right on Wiswell Road. You'll pass Copeland Hill Cemetery. In a little less than a mile, turn left onto Fields Pond Road. Drive about 1 mile. Fields Pond Audubon Center will be on your left. Pick up a map of the trails in the center or from the wooden cubby on the right side of the nature trails kiosk.

GPS coordinates: 44.738936', -68.727754'

Maine Audubon acquired the 192-acre property that became the Fields Pond Audubon Center by bequest from the estate of Katherine Curran in 1994. The gift of land included 1,600 feet of lakeshore and a 22-acre island in Fields Pond, which has long been a popular place for locals to paddle, fish, and swim.

Snapping turtles are often seen near Fields Pond.

In 1998 Maine Audubon opened a "green" building on the property named the L. Robert Rolde Nature Center after the Bangor-born, nature-loving father of the lead donor for the building's construction. The Nature Center is now home to offices for Audubon staff, an art gallery, a taxidermy display of local wildlife, and a gift shop with nature books, toys, Maine-made gifts, bird feeders, and binoculars. Often public programs are held in the building or start there, then transition to the outdoors.

The walking trails on the property make up about 5 miles all together and vary in difficulty from easy to moderate. Trails near the Nature Center explore fields that the Audubon maintains for ground-nesting birds. These easy trails also visit a frog pond and lead to the shore of the 85-acre Fields Pond, which is known to be a great place to look for big snapping turtles.

In the summer of 2016, the Fields Pond Audubon Center had just started the process of planning a new trail that would trace the perimeter of the property. This trail will have an estimated length of 5 miles. At the time, there was no set date for its completion.

Maine Audubon offers dozens of year-round public programs for people of all ages, as well as day camps for children during the summer and February vacation. Fields Pond Audubon Center staff also travel to give educational programs at schools throughout the state.

"Our role is to help people of all ages to fall in love with nature, whatever that might look like," said Cindy Kuhn, lead educator for Maine Audubon, in August 2016. "My role is finding ways to open the door for people to get outdoors."

Signs mark the intersections in the trail network at Fields Pond Audubon Center.

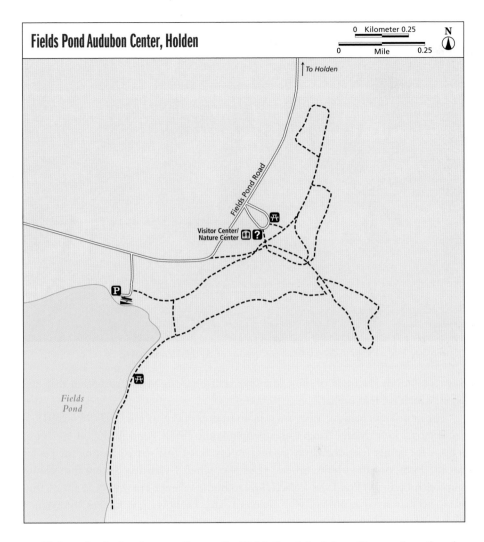

0   Kilometer 0.25

0   Mile   0.25

N

To Holden

Fields Pond Road

Visitor Center/
Nature Center

P

Fields
Pond

Kuhn, who is also the coordinator for Fields Pond Audubon Center, describes the trails at the center as "intimate" and narrow.

"It feels like you're sharing space with nature as opposed to blazing through a path," she explained.

The center has a number of nesting boxes and bird feeders that attract many species of birds to the property year-round, and the meadows and gardens around the Nature Center also attract a wide range of pollinators, such as butterflies. Then, in the property's mixed upland forest, barred owls are frequently sighted and more often heard.

"We have a huge variety of habitats throughout," Kuhn said. "We have wetlands, deciduous forest, mixed conifer forest, meadows, and riparian lakeside habitat . . . We

Narrow bog bridges help walkers over soggy sections of the Holden property.

have a textbook example of the many diverse habitats in Maine, all within that 200 acres, which is pretty stellar."

For more information: Visit www.maineaudubon.org or call (207) 989-2591.

Personal note: Many Bangor-area people know Fields Pond Audubon Center as a place for family friendly, nature-related events. But I first started visiting the center for the birds, not the events. Several years ago, when I was first getting into nature photography, Fields Pond was a place close to home where I knew I could always find birds, no matter what time of year. Bluebirds, tree swallows, goldfinches, nuthatches, blue jays, chickadees, cardinals—the list goes on and on.

Then, over the years, I started attending some of the events at Fields Pond, including a presentation on snowy owls, some of which fly down to spend the winter in Maine after breeding in the Arctic tundra. The presentation was given by Erynn Call, a knowledgeable raptor biologist for the Maine Department of Inland Fisheries, with photographs by Sharon Fiedler, a wildlife photographer from Bangor whom I've become friends with over the past few years through our mutual love for local wildlife and photography.

A lot of the programs at Fields Pond are designed for children, but there are a handful of events each year—such as the snowy owl presentation—that are more suited for attentive adults. And while most of the programs focus on nature, there are a few programs that are more geared toward outdoor recreation. For example, the center offers snowshoeing clinics and guided snowshoe activities every winter.

I visited in the winter once, but on that particular occasion, there was more ice than snow on the ground. I remember navigating the trails with my husband Derek, both of us with ice cleats fastened to our boots. That day in February, two ice shacks sat on the frozen pond, and the cattails in the marsh were stiff with ice.

But it was during another visit to Fields Pond that I had my most exciting experience on the property. In April 2013 I was there to photograph the tree swallows nesting in the meadows, and while walking near the cattail marsh, I spooked two white-tailed deer, one of them not 10 feet from me. They'd been walking through the cattails and tall grasses and hadn't seen me until I was almost right on top of them. I don't know who was more startled, them or me.

Hike 21 : Torsey Pond Nature Preserve in Readfield

About these trails: Featuring a mile of shoreline, significant wading bird habitat, and mixed forest uplands, Torsey Pond Nature Preserve is one of the richest biological areas in Readfield, according to the Readfield Conservation Commission. The 92-acre preserve is owned and managed by the town of Readfield, which purchased the land in 2001 with funds from the Maine Land and Water Conservation Fund, a town appropriation, and local contributions. The preserve offers about 2 miles of trails that travel through mixed forest to the edge of Torsey Pond.

Difficulty: Easy to moderate. The terrain is fairly level. Footing may be tricky in some areas because of exposed tree roots and long, narrow bog bridges.

Dogs: Permitted if on leash or under voice command. Carry out all pet waste.

Cost: Free, but donations can be made to the trail maintainer, Kennebec Land Trust, at www .tklt.org/donate.

Access: Open for day use year-round. Camping, fires, littering, smoking, bikes, and motorized vehicles are not permitted. Trails are for walking, cross-country skiing, and snowshoeing. Fishing and paddling are allowed on the pond. Canoe or kayak access is available from a public boat launch at the south end of Torsey Pond on Old Kents Hill Road.

Wheelchair accessibility: The trails were not constructed to be wheelchair accessible. They include narrow bog bridging and other objects that may be obstacles to wheelchairs.

Hunting: Prohibited, except for hunting waterfowl from the pond.

Restrooms: None.

How to get there: From the intersection of Route 17 and Route 41 (Chimney Road) in Kents Hill, go 1 mile north on Route 41 to the preserve's small gravel parking lot on the right. The trailhead is at the far end of the parking area.

GPS coordinates: 44.418384', -70.001066'

In 2003 Kennebec Land Trust accepted the land as a conservation easement, to be permanently protected for wildlife and recreation, and since then, the land trust has constructed approximately 2 miles of walking trails on the property.

The trail network is easy to navigate because each trail is marked with a different color of paint. Visitors enter the trail network on the Yellow Trail, which is marked with yellow blazes. The Yellow Trail leads to the Orange, Blue, and Green Trails. There is also the Red Trail, which forms a short bridge between the Blue and Green Trails.

A wildlife observation blind—a small wooden shelter with a partially open front—is located near the intersection of the Green and Orange Trails, at the edge of Torsey Pond. Hidden in the blind, visitors can watch a variety of wildlife, including loons, geese, ducks, and a number of migratory songbirds, depending on the time of year.

The majority of the trail network travels through mixed woodland. The upland portion was cleared for pasture in the 19th and 20th centuries, according to the

A group of geese are seen from the wildlife observation blind on the edge of Torsey Pond.

Kennebec Land Trust. Today, the forest has moved back in and includes a mix of hardwoods and conifers, including white pine, poplar, birch, and red maple.

In the forest you can find a diversity of wildflowers, including a large population of trout lilies, a yellow, six-petaled flower that grows in the forests of the eastern United States and Canada and blooms in the early spring. Its name refers to similarity between the lily's brown-mottled leaves and the patterns on a brown or brook trout.

The Blue Trail and Orange Trail both visit the edge of Torsey Pond, which was originally called Bean Mill Pond, then Greely Pond. In 1892 it was renamed in honor of Henry P. Torsey, an ardent fisherman and the headmaster at Kents Hill School in Readfield in the mid-1800s.

Today's Torsey Pond is combination of the original natural pond and a man-made section of the pond, according to the Torsey Pond Association. The natural pond began to expand in 1770, when a man named James Craig constructed a dam at the pond's present dam site and began operating a sawmill. The foundation of this sawmill is visible across Old Kents Hill Road from the existing dam. The pond now covers an area of 770 acres. It's long and irregular in shape, extending north to south about 2.5 miles, from the inlet at Tingley Brook to the outlet at the dam on Old Kents Hill Road.

Torsey Pond Nature Preserve is just one of the many preserves held by the Kennebec Land Trust, a nonprofit organization established in 1988. To date the land trust has partnered with landowners in 21 communities in central Maine to protect more

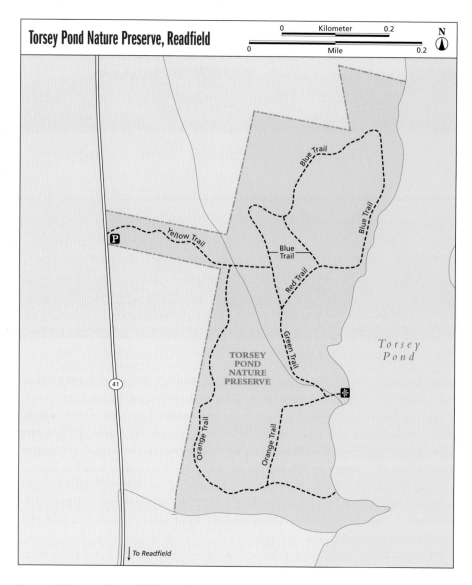

than 4,660 acres for wildlife and low-impact outdoor recreation, and the land trust has constructed 32 miles of trails for the public to enjoy.

For more information: Visit www.tklt.org or call the Kennebec Land Trust at (207) 377-2848.

Personal note: I visited Torsey Pond Nature Preserve for the first time during the spring, when the forest and pond were teeming with migratory birds. Even with my dog Oreo in tow, I saw a diversity of wildlife while walking the preserve's well-marked and well-maintained trails.

A group of Canada geese swim with their young on Torsey Pond.

I found the most luck while sitting at the wildlife observation blind at the edge of Torsey Pond. With Oreo sitting on the wooden floor of the blind, distracted by treats, I observed the sunny world outside, first with my eyes, then with my camera. Flitting through the underbrush along the edge of the pond, I spotted bright yellow warblers (they're hard to miss), and perched on swaying cattails were a number of red-winged blackbirds. Now and again, these beautiful birds would open their sharp beaks and let out piercing cries, then take flight, displaying bands of bright red and yellow feathers on their outstretched wings.

Out on the open water, a gaggle of Canada geese swam, their heads swiveling to and fro on their long, dark necks. At first I saw only adult geese. They're such large birds, with an average wingspan of about 5 feet. Then, I saw them—the tiny, fuzzy, yellow baby geese (also known as goslings) that the adults seemed to be herding along.

I eventually pulled myself away from the observation blind and explored the rest of the trail network, which traveled through a beautiful mixed forest filled with ferns and other native woodland plants.

I was so impressed by Oreo's good behavior during the wildlife photography session that, after the hike, we went for ice cream at a nearby convenience store. I ordered him the normal dog flavor, vanilla, while I opted for maple walnut. Then we sat on the front lawn outside the store to enjoy our cold treat, and for some reason, Oreo would only eat his ice cream if I fed it to him with a spoon. Of course, being the dog mom I am, I did just that, which may have attracted a few weird looks from people at the nearby gas pumps.

Hike 22: Witherle Woods Preserve in Castine

About these trails: The 185-acre Witherle Woods Preserve, owned by the Maine Coast Heritage Trust, features more than 4 miles of easy trails that are ideal for walking, snowshoeing, cross-country skiing, and mountain biking. The preserve was named after Castine resident George H. Witherle (1831–1906), who owned much of the property during the late 1800s.

Difficulty: Easy to moderate. The main trails in the 4.2-mile network are wide and smooth and travel over fairly even terrain. Some of the side trails are a bit more challenging.

Dogs: Permitted but must be kept under control at all times. Carry out all pet waste.

Cost: Free, though donations to the trail maintainers, Maine Coast Heritage Trust, can be made at www.mcht.org.

Access: The trails are open during daylight hours year-round. Camping and fires are not permitted. Motorists are not permitted, and bicyclists are asked to be considerate of pedestrians and limit use to dry conditions and appropriate trails. All visitors should remain on established trails. Do not remove archaeological artifacts; metal detectors are prohibited.

Wheelchair accessibility: The trails were not constructed to be wheelchair accessible. The vast majority of those miles are old roadbeds, however, and pretty flat and well maintained.

Hunting: Only bow hunting is permitted on this property, and in accordance with state laws.

Restrooms: None. However, public restrooms are available nearby at the town dock at the end of Main Street.

How to get there: From the junction of Castine Road (Route 166) and the Shore Road (Route 166A) in Castine, follow Castine Road south 0.9 mile to the top of a hill. Continue right at a sharp bend in the road, which becomes Battle Avenue. Drive 0.8 mile on Battle Avenue, then turn right into a gravel parking lot. Park close to the fence so you don't block the gate. Continue around the gate on foot, climbing a hill on a gravel road, and you'll soon come to an information kiosk on the right, just before the town reservoirs. At the kiosk you'll find a preserve map, guidelines, a registration log, and preserve brochures.

GPS coordinates: 44.386411', -68.811155'

An avid outdoorsman, George H. Witherle was a member of the Appalachian Mountain Club and known for his explorations of Katahdin in Baxter State Park, which he climbed at least nine times. On the property that is now Witherle Woods Preserve, he maintained carriage roads, providing a place for rusticators and year-round residents to walk, drive their carriages, and picnic. At the time, the land was known as Witherle Park and was mostly open meadow.

Atop Witherle Hill—the peninsula's highest point at 218 feet above sea level—Witherle constructed an 80-foot observation tower, which was consumed in a 1903 fire that burned about half his land (along with several nearby summer homes and the Dome-of-the-Rock Hotel at Dyce Head).

Over the years, the property changed hands. First, George Witherle's daughter Amy inherited the park. She then willed it to her cousin Anna Witherle, who sold it

A side trail of Witherle Woods Preserve trail network leads to a bench and a view of the Penobscot Bay.

to Francis W. Hatch Jr., who passed it on to his son, Frank Hatch—a longtime board and council member of the Maine Coast Heritage Trust. The land was then obtained by the land trust in four parcels over 21 years, forming what is now called Witherle Woods Preserve.

Today, the preserve is a place for local residents and visitors to the region to unwind, pick berries, and view wildlife. From the preserve's small parking area off Battle Avenue, a wide multiuse trail leads visitors to a trail network, which threads through forests and meadows to steep ledges on the coast and views of Penobscot Bay.

Throughout the trail network are signs that point out where military fortifications used to stand during the Revolutionary War and the War of 1812. Nothing of these structures is left for visitors to view today, but early maps show that a blockhouse was constructed near the summit of Witherle Hill, and another blockhouse, along with two semicircular earthwork batteries, was located along the steep bluff of Blockhouse Point. All of this was confirmed by an archaeological survey done between 2001 and 2003.

Over the past decade the woods have experienced a high level of mortality due to old age and insect damage. After storms in 2007 and 2008 caused major blowdowns, the trust worked with a forester and logger to salvage the timber, ensure public safety, and prepare for a healthy future forest. This changing landscape opened up a lot of different types of habitats for birds and other wildlife, as well as a variety of plants. An ecological study updated in 2010 found 195 plant species on the preserve; and a 2009

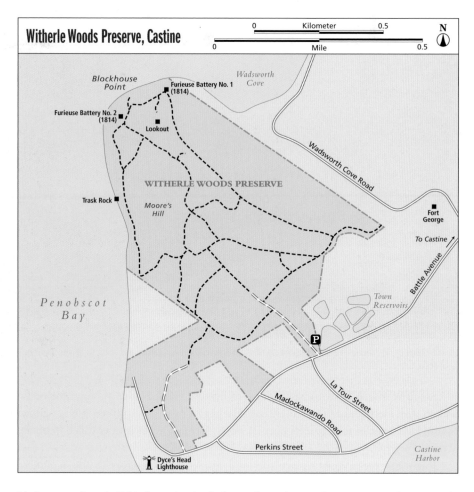

Witherle Woods Preserve, Castine

Blockhouse Point
Furieuse Battery No. 1 (1814)
Wadsworth Cove
Furieuse Battery No. 2 (1814)
Lookout
Wadsworth Cove Road
WITHERLE WOODS PRESERVE
Trask Rock
Moore's Hill
Fort George
To Castine
Battle Avenue
Penobscot Bay
Town Reservoirs
P
La Tour Street
Madockawando Road
Perkins Street
Castine Harbor
Dyce's Head Lighthouse

bird survey found 48 bird species, including white-throated sparrow, northern parula, black-throated green warbler, and winter wren.

For more information: Visit www.mcht.org or call Maine Coast Heritage Trust at (207) 729-7366.

Personal note: As I walked the trails of Witherle Woods Preserve on a particularly balmy day in mid-August, I stopped every now and again to carefully pluck a few ripe blackberries from a thorny mass of bushes bordering the trails. My dog Oreo wasn't interested in the late summer fruit, but he waited, panting in the hot sun, and whining when I stopped for too long. As usual, he wanted to see what was around the next bend.

Wildflowers and birds and berries—these are the things we typically found around each next bend. One of my favorite sights was a group of cedar waxwings, which were hard to miss, with their flashy yellow tail feathers and high-pitched calls.

I eventually navigated to the coast, where we found a bench atop a cliff (or perhaps it's more accurate to call it a very steep slope). There we sat and enjoyed the

Sun filters through trees lining a trail in the preserve.

Wild blackberries are ripe on bushes along many of the trails in the preserve in late August.

slightly cooler, salty breeze of the ocean. Over the tops of spruce and white birch trees growing below, we could see Penobscot Bay shimmering in the sun.

From there we took a different route back, which was easy, since the network is made up of so many intersecting trails. Most of the trails are wide, meaning they're open to the sun during the middle of the day. Because of this, Oreo and I were often looking for shade, and we stopped several times to drink water. It was also a necessity to go for ice cream after the hike.

Hike 23: Piscataquis County Demonstration Forest in Williamsburg Township

About these trails: The 180-acre Piscataquis County Demonstration Forest is a certified tree farm in the American Tree Farm System and features about 2.5 miles of interpretive trails open to the public year-round. Among the many highlights of the trail network are the remains of two large homesteads, a beautiful stand of tall red pines, and a canyon formed by a glacier thousands of years ago.

Difficulty: Easy to moderate, depending on how much of the trail network you choose to explore. The trails total about 2.5 miles.

Dogs: Permitted but must be kept on leash at all times. Visitors are expected to pick up after their dogs and dispose of waste properly.

Cost: Free.

Access: The trails are for foot traffic only. Bikes are not allowed. In the winter the parking area is not plowed, but the road leading to the forest entrance is plowed. Visitors can park to the side of the road, out of the way of traffic. Cross-country skiing and snowshoeing are permitted.

Wheelchair accessibility: The trails are not designed to be wheelchair accessible. The trails travel over forest floor that includes roots and rocks that would obstruct most wheelchairs.

Hunting: Allowed on a limited basis by permission.

Restrooms: There are two wooden outhouses, one near the main entrance and the other by the outdoor classroom.

How to get there: From Route 11 in downtown Brownville, turn onto High Street, which might not be marked with a sign but is across the street from Church Street and Robinson's Mobil store. On High Street drive 4.4 miles. You'll travel up Brown Hill and past the Moses Greenleaf monument, and the road will change to Williamsburg Road. At 4.4 miles the pavement ends and a road veers off to the right. Stay straight, continuing on Roberts Road (now dirt) for about 1 mile to Piscataquis County Demonstration Forest parking area, which will be on your right.

GPS coordinates: 45.368944', -69.089140'

Located in Williamsburg Township, the forest is maintained by the Piscataquis County Soil and Water Conservation District, which leads tours on the property about forest management practices, soil and water conservation, vernal pools, and other topics, according to the Piscataquis County Tourism Development Authority.

The trails on the property are fairly wide and smooth, forming three loops great for hiking, snowshoeing, and cross-country skiing. Throughout the network are many colorful displays about forestry practices, local wildlife, and the history of the property. These displays include old photos provided by the Brownville Historical Society and illustrations by local children.

From the forest's small parking lot, a wide path leads to the trailhead kiosk, where a detailed trail map is located. Beyond the kiosk is a clearing that serves as an outdoor classroom, and nearby is the historic site of the Decker and Lovejoy Homestead, built

THE LARSON/DECKER HOMESTEAD
Jansen Historical Society State

• The Decker family purchased this land in 1867 and built a homestead, barn/outbuildings shortly thereafter.

• Sten Larson, from Sweden, purchased this property with his new wife Gladys in 1905. He ran the grain store in Brownville and they raised sixteen children here at the Homestead.

The Larson Family

• The U.S. Forest Service owned and managed this land from 1946 until it was deeded to the Conservation District in 1980.

NORTH TRAIL LOOP

An interpretive display about the Larson and Decker Homestead, built in the 1860s, is one of the many interpretive displays located along the trails of the demonstration forest.

in the 1800s. All that remains today are the foundations and an old well, both marked with interpretive signs. (The well has been covered for safety.)

To the right of the trailhead kiosk, just beyond the gate, is where the trail network begins. All trails are marked with blue blazes and signs posted on tree trunks.

You'll start your hike on the Decker Trail, which soon leads to the Shelterwood Trail, a loop that visits a variety of tree harvest sites, including an area where precommercial thinning of softwood has been conducted and an example of shelterwood harvesting, a silvicultural technique used to naturally reseed and grow the next forest while retaining part of the old forest. Interpretive displays along the loop explain these forestry methods.

Branching off the Shelterwood loop is the Canyon Trail, which travels through a canyon that is approximately 70 feet deep and 200 feet wide and contains a variety of hardwood trees, as well as an example of a nursery log—a large fallen tree on which other trees and plants sprout as the wood decays—and a geocache site. Interpretive signs point out and explain these features along the trail.

Climbing out of the canyon, the Canyon Trail meets the Plantation Loop, which travels through a beautiful stand of red pine trees planted on a 12-acre field in 1957 as a timber crop. The tall, straight trunks of the pines are covered with rough, red-tinged bark, and the trees' long needles litter the forest floor.

Interpretive signs located along the trail state that homesteaders settled the region in the late 1800s, clearing the land for farming and building house foundations with

A stand of red pines planted by a farmer in 1957 and 1958 cover a 12-acre section of the demonstration forest.

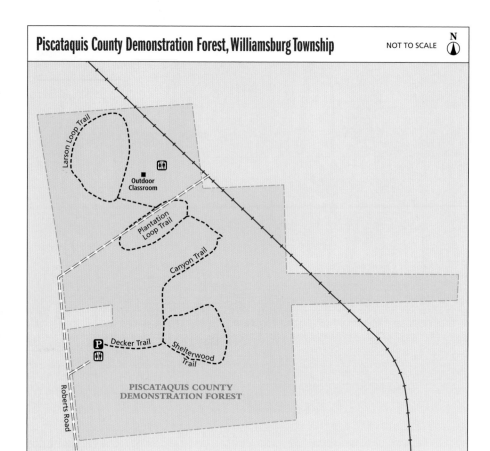

granite quarried nearby. At the north end of the Plantation Loop are the remains of the historic Larson and Decker Homestead, and nearby is a short side trail that leads to a clearing dotted with apple trees. This open area provides a great view to the north of Saddleback, Jo-Mary, and Ebeemee Mountains. A large pavilion was recently constructed at this vista so that visitors can take shelter, sit at a picnic table, and take in the view.

Continuing on, the final loop of the trail network is the Larson Loop, which visits an old hemlock growth and examples of new and old clear-cuts.

In 2007 the Piscataquis County Soil and Water Conservation District was awarded two national awards from the Maine Association of Conservation Districts for its work in the demonstration forest, and the Maine Audubon Society lists the forest in its Maine Birding Trails directory.

Though all trails are marked with signs, it's best to carry a trail map with you the first couple times you visit the property. Maps are available at the Piscataquis County Soil and Water Conservation District Office at 42 Pine Crest Drive in Dover-Foxcroft. Another option is to photograph the trail map posted on the trailhead kiosk. The

A clearing in the forest provides a view to the north off Saddleback, South Jo-Mary and Ebeemee Mountains.

interpretive displays are numbered, so you can use them to figure out where you are on the map if you get lost.

For more information: Call the Piscataquis County Soil and Water Conservation District Office at (207) 564-2321 or visit www.piscataquisswcd.org.

Personal note: A thin layer of fresh snow covered Bangor, the hub of holiday shopping madness, on December 16, when I escaped for a hike with my dog Oreo. As I drove north the landscape quickly changed. Snow clung to evergreens lining the road and piled up in the fields of Corinth and Charleston. By the time I reached Brownville, I was dealing with about 8 inches of fresh, white powder.

Just north of Brownville, Williamsburg Township seemed to be in the middle of nowhere. There were a few houses here and there, but for the most part, I was looking at trees and more trees as I drove to the Piscataquis County Demonstration Forest. As the road turned from paved to gravel, those trees closed in, some of them weighed down so much with snow and ice that they bowed into the road. Eventually, their icy branches blocked the way, and I was forced to park and continue on foot about 0.3 mile to the trailhead parking area.

As I snowshoed the trail network, Oreo bounded ahead on a long leash, often chest deep in snow but not seeming to mind. It was a sunny day, with the temperature reaching the mid-30s, causing melting snow to fall from the trees in sparkling streams. Before long Oreo's dog fleece was coated with clumps of sticky snow.

My favorite spot in the forest, by far, was the stand of red pines, planted by a farmer in 1957 and 1958 on what was a 12-acre field. There was something so peaceful about those tall, straight trees, their reddish trunks dusted with snow on one side and bare on the other, the sun filtering through their frozen branches high overhead.

When we reached the large wooden pavilion at the overlook beyond Plantation Loop, I took off my backpack, as well as Oreo's dog pack and coat, which was soaked. He was shivering. Fortunately, I had thought to pack a second dog coat. Once he had that on, he seemed much happier.

After a quick snack of granola bar (for me) and dog treats (for Oreo), we retraced our steps, jogging now and then to warm up. As we sped through the canyon and ducked under icy branches, clouds gathered and glowed pink in the darkening sky. By the time we reached the car, tiny snowflakes were falling.

Hike 24: South Bog Conservation Lands in Rangeley

About these trails: Rangeley Lakes Heritage Trust purchased the 1,000-acre South Bog Conservation Lands in 2004 to protect its natural resources and continue the land's long history as a working forest benefiting the local economy. In addition to valuable forestland—which today is managed as a Forest Stewardship Council–certified tree farm—the property includes extensive bog wetlands, ledge outcrops that offer views of Rangeley Lake, and South Bog Stream. About 2.5 miles of trails weave among these features.

Difficulty: Easy to moderate, depending on how much of the trail network you choose to tackle. The preserve's easy interpretive trail is 0.75 mile long and forms a loop that crosses South Bog Stream. The trail on the west side of the stream is easier, smoother, and wider than the trail on the east side of the stream. Branching off the interpretive trail is a 1.7-mile trail that is more challenging and leads to the shore of Rangeley Lake.

Dogs: Permitted if kept under control at all times. Carry out all pet waste.

Cost: Free, though donations can be made to the Rangeley Lakes Heritage Trust, which owns and maintains the property, at www.rlht.org.

Access: Trails are open to the public during daylight hours year-round; however, the parking lot is not plowed regularly in the winter. Fires and camping are not permitted. Trails are for foot traffic only. Bikes are not permitted.

Wheelchair accessibility: The trails were not constructed to be wheelchair accessible.

Hunting: Permitted, in accordance with state laws.

Restrooms: An outhouse is located near the trailhead.

How to get there: From Oquossoc Village drive south on Route 17 for 3.4 miles, then take a left onto South Shore Drive. Drive 2.2 miles and the parking area is on the left, just after South Bog Stream Bridge.

GPS coordinates: 44.914540', -70.705938'

This property can be explored by the public on about 2.5 miles of public hiking trails, which were constructed in 2009 and expanded and improved in 2012. These trails can be broken into two segments: the 0.75-mile interpretive trail, which follows the banks of South Bog Stream and forms a loop, and, branching off of the interpretive trail, a 1.7-mile trail that weaves through a mixed forest to the shore of Rangeley Lake.

Starting at the preserve parking lot on South Shore Drive, the interpretive trail enters the forest and follows along the east side of South Bog Stream to several scenic spots along the stream bank and two picnic spots, complete with picnic tables. This section of the trail is wide and smooth and includes several educational displays about the work that was done by the Maine Department of Inland Fisheries and Wildlife to restore the stream from 2004 to 2009.

My husband Derek and our dog Oreo walk along the interpretive trail in the preserve in June.

Originating on the north face of Four Ponds Mountain in western Maine, South Bog Stream flows just over 6 miles north to Rangeley Lake. Its cold water makes it an excellent habitat for wild brook trout, and to a lesser extent, landlocked salmon. A stream survey in 2011 indicated a lack of deep pools along the stream, which provide critical adult brook trout habitat. As a result, a program was undertaken in 2004 to restore pools to the stream through a variety of methods, including reshaping channels, placing root wads in gravel bars and outside banks to prevent erosion, and constructing structures with rocks and logs to narrow the channel and direct stream flow toward the center.

The interpretive trail also features displays about fisheries management, local wildlife, and woodland plants. For example, there is a display of interesting facts about brook trout. Did you know that brook trout bury hundreds of eggs in the gravel in the fall, and the eggs hatch in the spring?

Another interesting spot on the trail is a long wooden display on common native plants in the area. The display reads that Maine has 1,432 native plant species, with half of them considered rare and an additional 200 species that have been introduced to the state from other locations. Along the trail you can learn about some of Maine's tree species firsthand; identification tags fastened to tree trunks include each species' common and scientific names, a short description of the tree, and an illustration of its leaves.

At the far end of the loop, the trail crosses a shallow section of the stream on stepping-stones and loops around by traveling through the forest on the stream's west bank, back to South Shore Drive. This trail is narrower, with sections of bog bridges. At South Shore Drive turn left and walk along the road, crossing a bridge, to return to the trailhead and parking lot.

During the spring the water in the stream is often too high for people to cross. Nevertheless, visitors can still visit both sides of the interpretive trail from South Shore Drive.

Branching off the interpretive trail, on the stream's west side, a 1.7-mile trail leads through the forest, over somewhat hilly terrain to end at the south shore of Rangeley Lake. Just over halfway to the lake, the trail enters a field and splits into a loop. Veer left at this juncture and you'll climb up a steep hill to ledges overlooking the lake and surrounding forestland. If instead you turn right at this juncture, you'll hike over smoother terrain as you trace the bottom of the hill. At the far end of the loop, a single trail leads to the shore of the lake.

South Bog Conservation Lands is just one of the many properties owned and managed by the Rangeley Lakes Heritage Trust. Since its incorporation in 1991, RLHT has conserved more than 12,800 acres of land in the Rangeley Lakes region, including 45 miles of lake and river frontage, 15 islands, and the 2,443-foot Bald

Identification tags like this help visitors learn about a variety of trees throughout the trail network.

The trails of the preserve travel through a mixed forest where you can find a variety of native wildflowers.

Mountain. In addition to maintaining public hiking trails on many of their properties, RLHT staff members and volunteers work together to inspect boats for invasive plants and to inventory all the native aquatic plants in the region's lakes and ponds.

For more information: Visit www.rlht.org or call Rangeley Lakes Heritage Trust at (207) 864-7311.

Personal note: In early June I booked a cozy 1950s cabin in Rangeley for a weekend of outdoor exploration, reading, and relaxation with my husband Derek and our dog Oreo. After driving about 3 hours, we arrived in the western Maine town on Friday afternoon to find a clean, rustic cabin filled with the comforts of camp living—a woodstove, a screened-in porch, mismatching furniture, an old radio, a shelf full of books, and a closet full of board games.

Over the weekend the sun would refuse to shine but for a few minutes, but we didn't need perfect weather to enjoy the beauty of the region. Across three days we checked out five very different outdoor destinations, from easy bird walks to rugged mountain trails to one of Maine's tallest waterfalls. South Bog Conservation Lands was one of those places.

On Saturday morning, under a bright white sky, we started the day by walking the interpretive trail along the banks of South Bog Stream. I kept expecting the sun to break through the thin blanket of clouds overhead, but instead, it started to mist, then drizzle. Fortunately, the new leaves of spring created a bright green canopy overhead much of the way, keeping us relatively dry.

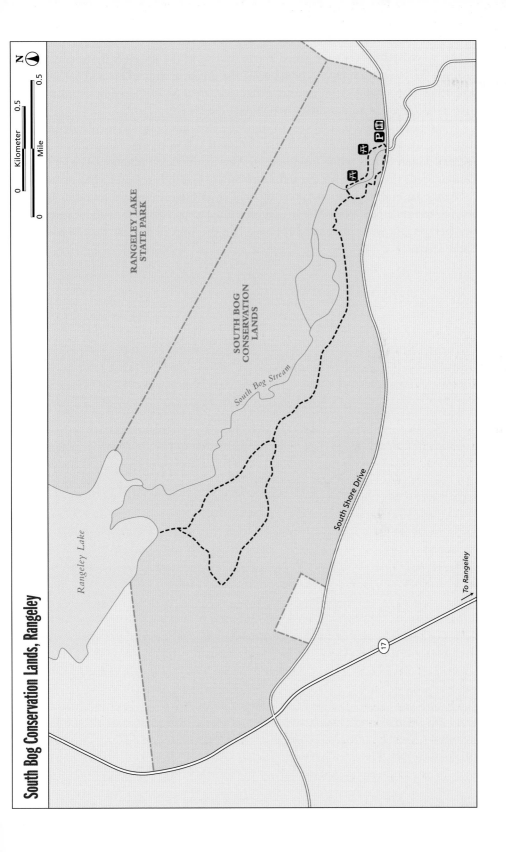

South Bog Conservation Lands, Rangeley

As we walked the trail, we passed a man wading in the stream, a fly-fishing rod in hand. We waved to him, and he returned the greeting with a curt nod, which is a perfectly respectful and enthusiastic greeting in rural Maine. Leaving the man in peace, we continued on our hike, Oreo leading the way.

It was just the right time of year to enjoy the blossoms of many woodland plants, including white, four-petaled bunchberry blossoms; yellow, trumpet-shaped trout lilies; and clusters of tiny white foam flowers. Also on the trail, I photographed an iridescent beetle that caught my eye and a garter snake as it slithered over a bed of moss.

At the far end of the loop, where the trail crosses the stream, we found it challenging to find a path across the stream on natural stepping-stones without getting our feet wet, but we managed and continued on the loop, all the way back to South Shore Drive.

Hike 25: Good Will-Hinckley Trails in Fairfield

About these trails: The construction of the Good Will–Hinckley Trails was started in the early 1900s by George Walter Hinckley, founder of Good Will–Hinckley Homes for Boys and Girls. Weaving through the forest and fields of Fairfield, the trails were for the children living at the Good Will–Hinckley Homes, as well as visitors to the property. He built them to encourage outdoor recreation and foster curiosity about the natural world.

Difficulty: Easy to moderate, depending on how many trails you choose to explore. The trails total over 3 miles and are well maintained and marked with blazes painted on trees. The surface of the trails is forest floor, which can be uneven and muddy in spots. Expect a few hills and short stretches of narrow bog bridges.

Dogs: Permitted if on leash at all times. Visitors are expected to pick up after their dogs and dispose of waste properly.

Cost: There is no fee to use the trails. Admission to the nearby L.C. Bates Museum is $3 for adults and $1 for children 17 years and younger.

Access: The trails are open to the public year-round. Bikes, motorized vehicles, fires, smoking, and camping are not permitted. The L.C. Bates Museum is open 10 a.m. to 4:30 p.m. Wednesday through Saturday, and 1 to 4:30 p.m. Sunday, April through September. During the winter the museum is open by appointment or by chance, so it's best to call ahead to ensure someone will be there. Also, visitors should dress warmly during the winter because the museum will be chilly.

Wheelchair accessibility: The trails were not built to be wheelchair accessible. Only part of the L.C. Bates Museum is wheelchair accessible. Call the museum for details.

Hunting: No.

Restrooms: A restroom is available in the L.C. Bates Museum when the museum is open, and a portable toilet is located near the trailhead April through November. Restrooms are also available in the nearby Good Will-Hinckley administration building on Prescott Drive.

How to get there: Starting at the intersection of Route 23 and Route 201 near the Hinckley Boat Launch (on the west end of a bridge over the Kennebec River) in Fairfield, drive south on Route 201 for about 1 mile and you'll see a sign for Kennebec Valley Community College, then signs for Good Will-Hinckley on your right. Continue on Route 201 for about 0.6 mile and turn right onto Easler Road, right after the big sign for the L.C. Bates Museum. Drive less than 0.1 mile to a small parking lot for the museum on the right. Park there and enter the museum for a trail map before exploring the trail network, which starts on the other side of Easler Road and is marked by a large trailhead kiosk. If you're facing the kiosk, the Dartmouth Trail starts to the left and leads into the trail network.

GPS coordinates: 44.662459', -69.626782'

"Oh, fair trails," starts the Good Will Trail Song, "I'll stroll beneath the shadows of thy leaf-laden arms and the joys of the woods shall be mine."

A building known as the Granite House was constructed in the early 1900s for the exhibition of Maine granites; Today, the trail network at Good Will-Hinckley leads to this building, which stands empty and open for visitors to explore.

Today, the trails in the network total more than 3 miles and visit several historical stone monuments, which are described in a brochure and marked on a trail map that is available at the nearby L.C. Bates Museum.

For new visitors, navigating this trail network may be difficult without a trail map. The four main trails of the network are marked with blazes of different colors: Dartmouth Trail has green and white blazes; Bowdoin Trail, black and white; Continental Trail, yellow and white; and Hennigar Trail, red and white. All side trails and connecting trails simply have white blazes.

The stone monuments located throughout the trail network include a stone throne originally constructed in 1912 by Ernest Thompson Seton, one of the founders of the Boy Scouts of America; a stone monument built in 1921 in honor of Theodore Roosevelt that includes a stone from the Roosevelt estate on Long Island; the Granite House, a stone and log cabin constructed by Charles D. Hubbard for the exhibition of Maine granites; and the Sunrise Fireplace, a stone fireplace built in 1933 in the middle of the forest.

The trails also lead to outdoor classrooms, beautiful stone archways, and memorials to people involved in conservation, outdoor education, and the studying of nature, such as Adirondack Murray, "Father of the Outdoor Movement."

The Dartmouth Trail Entrance for the Good Will-Hinckley Trails was built in 1915 with field-stone with funds from the Outing Club of Dartmouth.

"Memorials are valuable because: first, they take us into the past and show us why we should be grateful; second, they inspire us to emulate the examples memorialized; and third, they beckon us into the future," wrote George Hinckley in 1939.

The campus and mission of Good Will-Hinckley have changed over the years, but this has always been a place of learning and outdoor activity.

Today, the 1,000-acre campus includes a charter school called Maine Academy of Natural Sciences, the L.C. Bates Museum, the Glenn Stratton Learning Center, the Charles E. Moody School, and the 21st Century Community Learning Center.

The L.C. Bates Museum was constructed in the early 1900s by Hinckley, who was an avid collector of natural objects. One of the highlights of the museum is unique dioramas painted by Charles D. Hubbard, an outdoors enthusiast and plein air painter. These dioramas display a variety of taxidermized animals that are native to Maine. Hubbard aimed to depict specific areas of the state in the dioramas, and he went on-site to paint the backgrounds for each.

The museum also includes collections of Native American artifacts; a room devoted to the display of rocks, minerals, and fossils; classrooms and interactive nature displays for children; an old printing press and other antiques; a room filled with taxidermized birds, eggs, and bones; and a marine room that includes a fascinating seashell collection, mounted fish, and whalebones.

For children there is a museum scavenger hunt and a craft project available in the museum gift shop. The museum also provides tours, class field trips, traveling nature programs for classrooms, a full schedule of summer camps, birthday parties, and about 50 public nature programs annually.

For more information: Visit www.gwh.org/lcbates or call (207) 238-4350.

Personal note: My dog Oreo waited in the car as I walked up the snow-packed steps of the L.C. Bates Museum to the front doors of the great brick building. A sign posted on the large wooden doors flapped in the wind, and I grabbed it to make out the writing. "Use the side door," it instructed, so I descended the granite stairs with care and walked back across the soggy lawn, skirting patches of mud by the parking area to find a small wooden door at the side of the building. It was March, and I wasn't sure if the museum would be open. But I was there, so I figured, why not give it a try?

To my surprise, the door gave way, swinging into a dim, cold room. I stepped inside, and staring down at me was an antelope. It stood on a glass case, which was filled with wood blocks and pressed leaves. My focus widened, taking in rows of bleached animal skulls, turtle shells, and animals frozen in time through the art of taxidermy. There were black bear cubs wrestling, a bobcat baring its teeth, and a snake poised, ready to strike.

As I processed the odd surroundings, I almost tripped over a wooden chair placed just before the door. On it sat a brass bell and a sign instructing visitors to ring upon arrival. I picked it up and swung it back and forth lightly, breaking the silence with

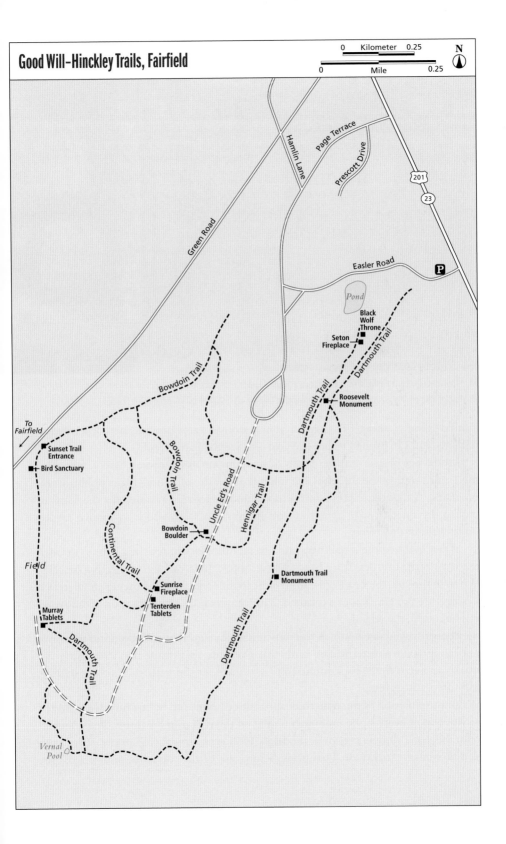

Good Will–Hinckley Trails, Fairfield

0   Kilometer   0.25

0   Mile   0.25

N

201
23

Hamlin Lane
Page Terrace
Prescott Drive
Green Road
Easler Road

P

Pond

Black
Wolf
Throne

Seton
Fireplace

Dartmouth Trail

Dartmouth Trail

Bowdoin Trail

Roosevelt
Monument

To
Fairfield

Sunset Trail
Entrance

Bird Sanctuary

Bowdoin Trail

Uncle Ed's Road

Hennigar Trail

Continental Trail

Bowdoin
Boulder

Dartmouth Trail
Monument

Field

Sunrise
Fireplace

Tenterden
Tablets

Murray
Tablets

Dartmouth Trail

Dartmouth Trail

Vernal
Pool

A plaque displaying a quote by Chaucer was donated by Wavus Camps in Jefferson, to be placed in one of the many stone monuments located along the Good Will-Hinckley Trails.

a timid "ding . . . ding." A cheerful young woman came around the corner almost instantly, and I explained to her my goal—to see the nature trails.

I soon was placed into the hands of museum curator Deborah Staber, who gave me a quick tour of the museum and told me about the museum's many public nature programs. A nighttime program on moths and meteorites planned for the summer piqued my interest, so I signed up for the museum's e-mail list to receive regular updates about the events.

Staber grabbed me a trail map and several other brochures, then led me through the day's craft: UV-detecting beads strung onto a pipe cleaner to create a bracelet. When in the sun, the beads turn from clear to different colors, showing children that UV rays are present, Staber explained. This can open up a conversation about wearing sunscreen, she added.

I could have spent hours in the museum, enjoying Hubbard's beautiful dioramas, inspecting taxidermized Maine birds that I've only seen from afar, and ogling the sparkly minerals in the rock room. But I was there for the trails, the sun was shining, and Oreo was waiting.

Our exploration of the trails took about three hours, and in that time we managed to visit almost every stone monument listed on the trail map brochure. Oreo climbed onto the stone throne known as the Black Wolf Seat, constructed in the early 1900s as a monument to Ernest Thompson Seton, one of the founding pioneers of Boy

Scouts of America and a visitor to Good Will-Hinckley. Oreo also sniffed around the Granite House, a beautiful stone building constructed designed by Charles D. Hubbard in the 1930s to display paintings of Maine stone quarries accompanied by samples of Maine granite. We walked down the Avenue of Pines and sat on a bench of an outdoor classroom for a snack. And the whole time, we saw not another soul, save for many chickadees and nuthatches and one pileated woodpecker that flew so close overhead it seemed to say hello.

Hike 26: Mingo Springs Nature Trail and Bird Walk in Rangeley

About this trail: Threading through a beautiful, varied forest and across lupine fields, the Mingo Springs Trail and Bird Walk is approximately 3 miles long and forms two loops around the front and back nine of the Mingo Springs Golf Course in the western Maine town of Rangeley.

Difficulty: Easy. The two loops are smooth and wide, and in many places they are surfaced with gravel or wood chips. Together, the two loops total about 3 miles.

Dogs: Permitted if they are kept on leash at all times. Carry out all pet waste and dispose of it properly.

Cost: Free.

Access: The trail is for foot traffic only. Bikes are not permitted.

Wheelchair accessibility: The trail was not constructed to be wheelchair accessible. While sections of the trail are smooth and wide, there are several obstacles, including narrow bridges and ditches.

Hunting: Not permitted.

Restrooms: Available in the nearby Mingo Springs Golf Course Pro Shop from mid-May through mid-October.

How to get there: From the intersections of Route 4 and Route 16 in downtown Rangeley, drive north (though technically west) on Route 4 for 2.3 miles and turn left onto Mingo Loop Road. Drive about 0.4 mile and turn left onto Alpine Way. Immediately on the left is the maintenance shed for Mingo Springs Golf Course. Park on the grass to the left of the building, by a white sign that reads "Trail parking."

GPS coordinates: 44.962105', -70.692830'

The creation of the trail was privately funded by the Chodosh family, which has owned and operated Mingo Springs Golf Course over the past 45 years, with three generations involved in running the facility.

Over the course of three years, from 2008 to 2010, the trail was constructed by the golf course grounds crew, under the leadership of John Bicknell, a golf course employee who also created many of the gardens on the property. Bicknell consulted with local foresters and naturalists to label plant species along the trail, especially trees and ferns.

In addition, wooden benches have been constructed at a few spots along the trail for visitors to rest and watch for the many different species of birds that live in the forest and fields, including a variety of warblers, vireos, woodpeckers, and owls.

In May 2016 Mingo Springs Golf Club achieved designation by Audubon International as a Certified Audubon Cooperative Sanctuary. As of summer 2016, it was one of four golf courses in Maine and 825 in the world to hold the title. The designation is achieved when a golf course meets specific standards of environmental management, which includes plans for water conservation, chemical use reduction, wildlife and habitat management, and outreach and education.

A lupine field is one of the main attractions of the Mingo Springs trails, with the lupines blossoming in June.

From the parking area, the trailhead is marked with a kiosk across Mingo Loop Road. At that location the two loops that make up the trail network meet. One loop is marked with red painted blazes, while the other loop is marked with blue. To start on the red loop, walk straight past the kiosk and into the woods. To start on the blue loop, turn right and walk along the road for a short distance until you see blue blazes.

The red-blazed loop is about 2 miles long and circles around the back nine holes of the golf course, through a hardwood forest and past a vernal pool, which is a haven and breeding ground for a variety of amphibians in the springtime. The trail then follows Mingo Loop Road for a short stretch before heading back into the woods to pass through a hardwood stand adjacent to a cedar swamp. After that it crosses old pastures that have been infiltrated by spruce and fir trees, then enters a stand of older evergreen trees.

Eventually, the trail comes out on Mingo Loop Road, which can be followed back to the parking area. Or you can choose to cross the road to hike the blue-blazed loop.

The blue-blazed trail is about 1 mile long and travels around the front nine holes of the golf course. This loop is especially popular during lupine season in June because it travels through two fields of lupines. This trail also passes through an evergreen forest and over a small hill. Be sure to follow the blue blazes and blue wooden arrows, as it is easy to get off-trail, especially where the trail passes over the groomed lawn by the golf clubhouse.

Signs label many types of ferns growing along the Mingo Springs trail.

Trail maps, restrooms, food, and beverages are available at the nearby Mingo Springs Golf Course Pro Shop from mid-May through mid-October. For the rest of the year, trail maps are available at the Rangeley Lakes Chamber of Commerce.

For more information: Call Mingo Springs Golf Course at (207) 864-5021 or visit www.mingosprings.com/trail-and-bird-walk.

Personal note: It was a dreary morning in June when I arrived at Mingo Springs Trail and Bird Walk with my husband Derek and our dog Oreo. Above all things I was there for the lupines, having heard about the golf course's beautiful lupine fields on a previous visit to the Rangeley Lakes region.

I was pleasantly surprised when I discovered that the trail offered much more than just a walk through lupine fields. The smooth, wide trail traveled through some stunning forestscapes, abundant with woodland flowers, and it was an excellent place to learn more about Maine plants. For instance, I knew about the cinnamon fern, which often grows near wetlands and is easy to identify with its cinnamon-colored stalk. And I also knew about ostrich ferns, which Mainers enjoy picking in the spring and tossing in a frying pan with butter. But on the trail I learned that there is a great variety of ferns that grow in Maine. There's the lady fern and oak fern, bracken fern and polypody fern, interrupted fern and narrow beech fern. All of these species were labeled on nice wooden signs posted throughout the trail.

There were also signs pointing out the wide variety of trees that naturally grow on the landscape, including beaked hazelnut, northern white cedar, Scotch pine, white spruce, striped maple, balsam fir, and white birch.

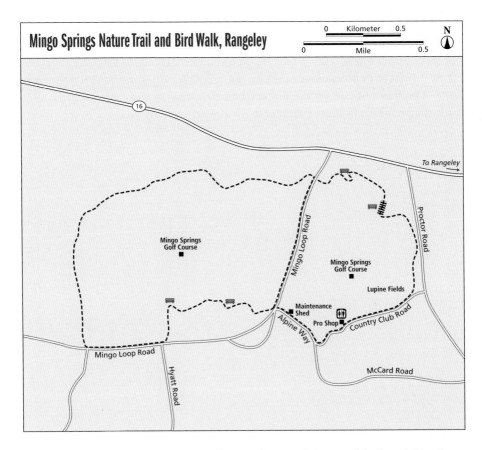

It being a bird walk, you're probably wondering what sort of feathered friends we encountered along the way, and we did manage to spy a few. In the woods, drilling in on tree trunks, was a yellow-bellied sapsucker, a woodpecker that drills rows of small holes in trees so it can lick up the sap that leaks out. This bird has a red cap and throat, with the rest of its body being a pattern of black and white, and as its name implies, it has a yellow-tinged belly.

Also, while I stopped to photograph the tiny, white, bell-shaped blossoms of a woodland flower called lily-of-the-valley, Derek witnessed two blackburnian warblers get into a bit of an aerial tussle, which caused them both to nearly land on top of me as they fell from the sky and onto the mossy forest floor. After the event they flew up into the trees, seemingly unharmed, and I spent the next 10 minutes or so trying to photograph these flashy birds as they flew from branch to branch, their yellow-orange feathers standing out against the greens and browns of the mossy evergreen forest.

And what we didn't see, we heard. The forest was alive with birdsong that day, including one of my favorites—the sweet song of the hermit thrush.

By the time we reached the lupine fields, we were nearing the end of our hike, and it started to rain. Derek raced through the fields with Oreo and ducked back into the cover of the forest, while I lingered in the lupines, trying to keep the raindrops off my camera as I photographed the blue, purple, pink, and white flowers from every angle. The drops of rain on the lupines' bulbous petals and fanned-out leaves only made the photographs more beautiful in my opinion, adding vibrance to the colors.

Hike 27: Range Pond State Park in Poland

About these trails: Featuring wide sandy beaches on the scenic Lower Range Pond, Range Pond State Park has long been a popular place for the public to enjoy watersports, picnicking, sunbathing, and fishing. In recent years the park has expanded its network of walking and biking trails and has started opening its gates year-round to offer a wider range of outdoor activities during all seasons.

Difficulty: Easy. The park's 1-mile nature trail is easy enough for young children.

Dogs: Permitted on the trails if kept on a leash no longer than 4 feet at all times. Dogs are not permitted on the beaches between April 1 and September 30; they are permitted on the beaches during the rest of the year. Visitors are expected to pick up after their dogs and dispose of waste properly.

Cost: Park admission is collected at the gate year-round. If an attendant isn't present, leave admission in the metal canister at the gate. Admission for Maine residents is $6 for adults, $1 for children ages 5–11, and free for children under 5 and seniors (65+). For nonresidents, adults are $8, children 5–11 are $1, seniors (65+) are $2, and children under 5 are free.

Access: Park hours are 9 a.m. to sunset daily unless otherwise signed at the gate, which is open year-round.

Wheelchair accessibility: Much of the park is wheelchair accessible, including the first part of the nature trail, the picnic tables, and a boat launch.

Hunting: Not permitted between June 1 and Labor Day. During all other times, hunting is permitted in accordance with state laws and local ordinances. However, the discharge of any weapon is prohibited from or within 300 feet of any picnic area, camping area or campsite, parking area, building, shelter, boat launch site, posted trail, or other developed area.

Restrooms: Restrooms and changing rooms are located between the main parking lot and the beach. Also, vault toilets are located throughout the park. The restrooms with plumbing are closed during the winter, but the vault toilets remain open for visitors to use.

How to get there: The park is located off Empire Road in Poland. From Interstate 95, take exit 75 and drive south on Route 202 for 1 mile, passing Crossroads Market and Southern Maine Auto Auction, then turn right onto Route 122 (Poland Spring Road). Drive 0.8 mile to a stop sign, then turn left onto Route 122 (Hotel Road). Drive 3 miles, then turn right onto Empire Road. Drive 0.7 mile, then turn left onto State Park Road, which is marked with a large sign for Range Pond State Park. Drive about half a mile to the main parking area, stopping at the entrance booth on the way to pay admission.

GPS coordinates: 44.038146', -70.342092'

"We're trying to promote the park as more than just a beach," said Range Pond State Park manager Adam McKay during a phone interview in March 2016.

Range Pond State Park was established in the mid-1960s, when the state of Maine purchased most of the 740 acres of the land for the park from Hiram Ricker and Sons, bottlers of Poland Spring Water. Now a division of Nestle Waters North America, the Poland Spring Bottling Company still bottles water at a plant beside the park and

An interpretive display stands at the beginning of the interpretive nature trail at Range Pond State Park.

maintains a partnership with the Maine Department of Conservation's Bureau of Parks and Lands, which operates Range Pond State Park.

The park's amenities include a playground, picnic areas, restrooms, a group shelter, seasonal lifeguards, and a boat launch limited to 10-horsepower motors.

For visitors looking to stretch their legs, a wide, surfaced promenade parallels the pond for 1,000 feet next to the park's Main Beach, and easy trails branch off it, totaling about 5 miles of walking.

Among those trails is a mile-long nature trail that is easy enough for young children and includes numbered interpretive displays that help visitors better understand the park's natural features, wildlife, and history. Starting at an interpretive display at the south end of South Beach, the nature trail travels south through the woods on a wide gravel path, passing a wetland on the way to the small, sandy Frenchman's Beach. From there the nature trail leads to a scenic overlook atop a hill formed out of a glacial deposit, then the trail loops around a wetland through a quiet mixed forest.

The interpretive displays located along the trail include text, diagrams, and photos of local wildlife and plants. Topics covered in the displays include the water cycle and watersheds, the glacial and human history of the property, and the history and science behind Poland Spring mineral water. And when you're done with your walk, be sure to stop by the park drinking fountain for a drink of the famous Poland water.

At the north end of the park, starting at the north end of the main beach, are more easy walking trails, including a 2-mile loop that is groomed for cross-country

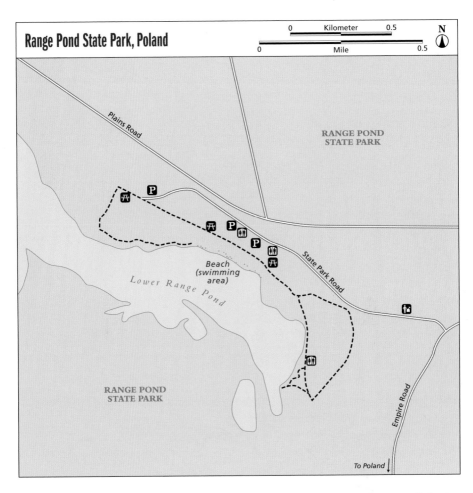

Range Pond State Park, Poland

Plains Road

RANGE POND
STATE PARK

Lower Range Pond

Beach
(swimming
area)

State Park Road

RANGE POND
STATE PARK

Empire Road

To Poland

skiing during the winter, and a 1.5-mile loop that serves as a multiuse trail during the winter.

In addition, the park features about 5 miles of single-track mountain biking trails that are easy enough for beginners.

For more information: Call the park at (207) 998-4104 or visit www.maine.gov/ rangepond.

Personal note: It was starting to feel like spring on April 25, 2016, when I arrived at Range Pond State Park and sat down in the sand of the park's Main Beach. Looking out to the sparkling water of Lower Range Pond, I watched a kayaker slice through small waves as he worked his way toward the dock. And farther off, a group of fishermen had linked their two canoes; together they drifted, casting lines into the deep blue water.

It being a weekday and so early in the year, the park was fairly quiet, though I understand it can get very busy during summer weekends. On the beach a family played in the sand, and a few dog walkers passed by on the easy trails nearby.

An easy nature trail forms a 1-mile loop in the park and includes a number of interpretive displays to help visitors learn more about the geology and wildlife of the park.

A gull floats near the shore of Lower Range Pond in late April.

After a while soaking in the sun, I reluctantly rose to my feet to walk the park's interpretive nature trail, which led to a scenic overview of a wetland, where I counted 10 eastern painted turtles basking on logs.

After my walk I returned to Main Beach and found it empty, so I sat down in the soft sand once more and simply enjoyed the sun, then wandered a bit, stopping every now and again to inspect freshwater snail and mussel shells—which were much lighter than the shells I find along the Maine coast. According to the Department of Inland Fisheries and Wildlife, Maine is home to 10 native species of freshwater mussels, 3 of which are currently listed as threatened under the Maine Endangered Species Act.

Also buried in the sand of Range Pond State Park were rocks of different colored granite and flecks of mica—a shiny, layered mineral that almost looks like glass and causes the mountains of western Maine to sparkle in the sun.

Hike 28: Sandy Point Beach Park in Stockton Springs

About these trails: Sandy Point Beach Park is located on French's Point, where the Penobscot River flows into the ocean. This beautiful place—with sand and rock beaches, a quiet fern-filled forest, and about 2 miles of walking trails—has a rich and varied history.

Difficulty: Easy. The trail network is made up of about 2 miles of trails and there is no significant change in elevation. On the Amazon Trail and Shore Trail, expect long sections of narrow bog bridges and watch out for exposed tree roots.

Dogs: Permitted on or off leash but must be under owner's control at all times. Carry out all pet waste.

Cost: Free.

Access: The park is open for day use only. There are no lifeguards; visitors swim at their own risk. Small recreational fires are allowed only on the beach in the area directly in front of the parking lot, 20 feet away from any vegetation, and below the high tide line. The trails are for foot traffic and wheelchairs only. Motorized vehicles and bicycles are not permitted. The parking area is not plowed in the winter, but local residents continue to use the property in the winter by walking there.

Wheelchair accessibility: A part of the trail network was constructed to be wheelchair accessible. It's wide, surfaced with packed gravel, and about 0.3 mile long but may not meet ADA standards. Wheelchair users may need some assistance on this trail, which spans from the parking lot on Hersey Retreat Road to the beach parking lot at the end of Steamboat Wharf Road and out to a viewpoint and bench above the beach. Also, from the beach parking lot, a wheelchair-accessible boardwalk leads through the grass to a wooden platform by the beach where there are two wooden benches.

Hunting: Not permitted. However, it used to be permitted on the property, so the town advises that people wear blaze orange while enjoying the woodland trails, especially during fall hunting seasons.

Restrooms: A restroom is located at the trailhead parking lot on Hersey Retreat Road.

How to get there: From the intersection of Route 1 and Route 1A in Stockton Springs, take Route 1 (Route 3) northeast 2.1 miles and turn right onto Steamboat Wharf Road, which is just after Pirates Cove Road (also a right). Drive 0.4 mile and you'll come to an intersection with Hersey Retreat Road. Continue straight through the intersection, following Steamboat Wharf Road another 0.1 mile to the long, gravel parking lot for Sandy Point Beach. The trail network begins at the far end of the parking lot and is marked by a kiosk where a trail map is available and information about the park is posted. A second trailhead is located on Hersey Retreat Road, less than 200 feet south of where Hersey Retreat Road and Steamboat Wharf Road intersect.

GPS coordinates: 44.506459', -68.807442'

Artifacts found along the shoreline of French's Point indicate that it was once a summering and trading spot for Paleolithic people and, later, the Penobscot Native Americans. During the American Revolution a major naval battle took place in

Baby ospreys poke their heads out of a nest built on old pilings near Sandy Point Beach.

nearby waters, where 39 American vessels were lost. And during the 19th century, several shipyards that built schooners popped up along the point, and a sawmill bordered Sandy Point Beach's north end.

During World War I the US Department of War built a shipyard on the south side of the beach. And in the early 20th century, a passenger steamboat line made a stop there. The remains of its wharf can be seen midbeach at low tide. The more visible pilings (closer to the bay) are from a second pier constructed midcentury for a fertilizer plant that operated into the early 1970s. Today, osprey and other birds nest on these pilings.

Sandy Point Beach Park, a state property managed by the town of Stockton Springs, was established in 1990 when 96 acres were purchased with Land for Maine's Future funds. Eight additional acres were gifted by local residents in 2003.

After the park was established, a group of devoted community volunteers and a Maine Conservation Corps crew constructed a network of trails on the property. Together, these trails total about 2 miles. Many people visit the park simply to enjoy the long sandy beach and never think to explore these well-marked trails, which weave through the forest to several views of the river.

At the large beach parking lot, the trail network begins at the far end, by a trailhead kiosk. There a wide gravel trail leads through tall grasses, bushes, and wildflowers as it climbs a small hill and enters the forest. At the first trail juncture, you can turn left and follow the gravel trail to a bench at an overlook of the river. This is the perfect place to watch the local osprey nest, which is usually constructed atop the old pilings straight ahead.

Back at the trail juncture, if you turn right, the wide gravel trail will soon lead you to the parking lot on Hersey Retreat Road. Along the way is a wooden bridge to

The Shore Trail leads to a small, quiet beach at the park with great views of the water.

your left. Take this bridge to explore the more challenging Amazon Trail and Shore Trail, both of which form loops through the forest of French's Point.

The 1.1-mile Amazon Trail, marked with blue blazes, leads you to the west end of the park. The path is a traditional hiking trail, traveling over unimproved forest floor and over several long sections of narrow bog bridges. After crossing the gravel Hersey Retreat Road, the Amazon Trail splits into a loop.

At the far end of the loop is an intersection with the 0.5-mile Shore Trail loop, which is marked with white blazes and will lead you to a nice, private, rocky beach on the banks of the Penobscot River. It then loops back through the woods to reconnect with the Amazon Trail.

And last but not least, the 0.3-mile Crystal Lynn Trail spurs off from the far end of the Shore Trail and leads to the south end of Hersey Retreat Road.

This trail network may get confusing once you're out there, even though major intersections are marked with signs. It's always smart to carry a trail map.

Whether enjoying the beach or walking the trails, plan to carry out all of your trash and pick up any litter you find. There are no trash cans at the park. Also, visitors are asked to respect wildlife and leave plants for everyone to enjoy. Don't climb up or down the bluffs and banks along the shore, as that will likely hasten their erosion, and be sure to dismantle fire rings and rock art before leaving the park.

For more information: Call the Stockton Springs town office at (207) 567-3404.

Personal note: The seahorse pool floaty was an essential, my 4-year-old niece Willa assured me. As were the plastic bucket, shovel, sand molds, and a toy boat. Then

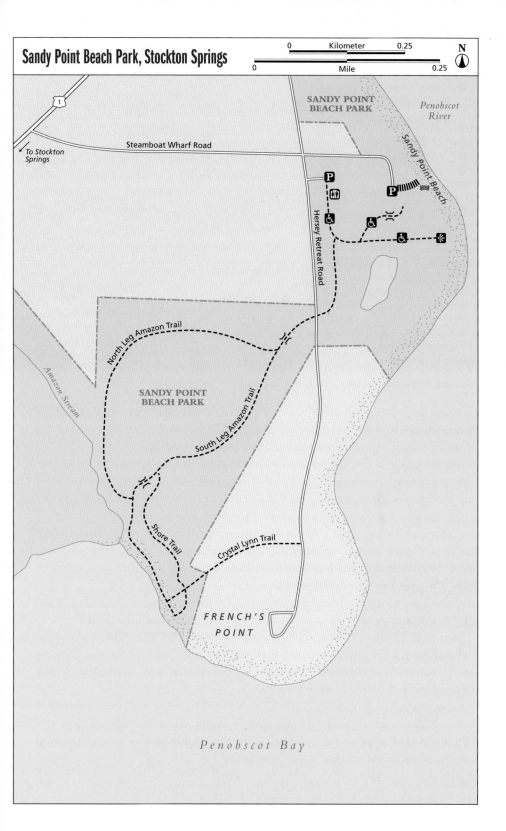

Sandy Point Beach Park, Stockton Springs

0   Kilometer   0.25
0   Mile   0.25

N

SANDY POINT
BEACH PARK

Penobscot
River

Steamboat Wharf Road

To Stockton
Springs

Sandy Point Beach

P

P

Hersey Retreat Road

North Leg Amazon Trail

SANDY POINT
BEACH PARK

South Leg Amazon Trail

Amazon Stream

Shore Trail

Crystal Lynn Trail

FRENCH'S
POINT

Penobscot Bay

My niece, Willamina, balances on a narrow bog bridge in the park's trail network.

there was the sunscreen, lunch box of snacks, water bottles, hats, extra clothes, and life jackets—though I doubted we'd be swimming. Willa said we needed it all, and I didn't object. I was just happy we were going on an adventure together.

As we walked across the hot sand of Sandy Point Beach—a place I used to visit with my family when I was a little girl—I struggled to keep a firm grasp on all of our unnecessary gear and instructed Willa to find a place for us to sit. Eventually, she chose a spot by the water, and I realized I'd forgotten towels.

That was all right, Willa told me. No one was perfect. We'd sit on the pool toys and extra clothes. And so we did. Willa filled her plastic bucket with salty water and made "potions" by dropping sparkly rocks from the beach into the water, counting them off—one, two, three sparkly rocks.

After a good long while making potions and rocky sand castles, I hauled all of the pool floaties and toys back to the car, and we set out on the trails of the park.

At first Willa didn't understand how I knew where to go. Then I pointed out the trail markers painted on the trees, and from that point on, Willa led the way, pointing out the blazes ahead. She especially liked how the different trails were marked with different colors. It all made sense.

That day, on the private beach off the Shore Trail, I carried Willa over a jumble of driftwood, then sat with her by the water. She'd never seen such a landscape. The soft, light green grasses rippling in the wind by the shore, and the river beyond, yawning into the Atlantic. She told me it was "wonderful."

Bunches of brown rockweed lined the shore, and Willa said she was scared of it—something she says about most things she has never seen before. So I grabbed a clump of the seaweed in my hands and tore open a bubble of it, letting the goo seep out. When I was a little girl, I told Willa, I used to soothe my scrapes with seaweed goo. Instantly, she wanted to try it. So we played doctor there on the beach, healing each other's wounds with seaweed.

These are the type of memories I'm blessed with for having spent just one afternoon at Sandy Point Beach Park with my niece. Back on the trails, we mimicked the call of birds we heard singing in the forest and paused to watch a chipmunk. Willa became more confident walking across narrow bog bridges, and by the end of our little hike, I noticed an improvement in her coordination as she marched along the trail.

While that trip to the park stands out in my mind as particularly special, I've been to the park many other times for other reasons. I've visited Sandy Point with my husband and dog to simply enjoy the water and sand. And I've also visited the park alone to photograph the resident ospreys, which have nested on old pilings offshore for many years now, raising their young each summer, then migrating south as the season wanes.

Hike 29: Bog Brook Cove Preserve in Cutler

About these trails: Located on the Bold Coast in eastern Maine, the 1,770-acre Bog Brook Cove Preserve is owned and maintained by the Maine Coast Heritage Trust and features about 5 miles of hiking trails for people of all skill levels. These trails visit cobblestone beaches, travel over a rocky ridge, and wind through a mixed forest to a freshwater pond and scenic outlooks along the rocky coast.

Difficulty: Easy to moderate, depending on the trails you choose to hike within the preserve. The Ridge Trail, accessible from the Trescott parking area, is the most challenging trail in the preserve; it's narrow, rocky, and steep in some sections. The 0.4-mile gravel trail leading from the Trescott parking area to the water is the easiest trail.

Dogs: Permitted if kept under control at all times. Carry out all pet waste.

Cost: Free.

Access: The preserve is open to the public year-round for day use. In the winter the south parking lot in Cutler is plowed; however, Moose River Road is usually plowed only halfway to the north parking lot in Trescott. Camping and fires are not permitted.

Wheelchair accessibility: The 0.4-mile gravel trail that starts at the Trescott parking area was constructed to be wheelchair accessible and ends at an overlook of the rocky coastline.

Hunting: Permitted, in accordance with state laws.

Restrooms: None.

How to get there: There are two parking areas for the preserve. The south parking area is in Cutler off Route 191, 5.5 miles north of the post office. Use this trailhead for Norse Pond Trail and Bog Brook Cove Beach. The north parking area is in Trescott. From the south parking area, drive 1.5 miles north on Route 191 and turn onto Moose River Road, which starts out paved, then turns gravel. Continue 1.1 miles and the parking area is at the end of the road. Use this trailhead for the wheelchair-accessible trail, beaches at Moose Cove, Chimney Trail, and Ridge Trail.

GPS coordinates: Trescott parking area: 44.731484', -67.101769'; Cutler parking area: 44.717078', -67.136704'

Of the two parking areas for the preserve, the south parking area provides access to the Norse Pond Trail, which starts out as a single trail, then splits into a loop that travels close to the north end of the 11-acre Norse Pond. At the far end of the loop trail, a side trail leads to Bog Brook Cove Beach. And another blazed trail travels north to Bog Brook, which it crosses to continue through the forest to the private, gravel Bog Brook Road.

The north parking area, located in Trescott Township, provides access to a wheelchair-accessible trail, which starts near the trailhead kiosk at the parking area and travels 0.4 mile to an overlook above a cobblestone beach. Lined with alders, grasses, and low-lying shrubs, the trail is a great place for bird-watching. And from the overlook at the end of the trail, you can look across the Grand Manan Channel

A black-and-white warbler perches in a tree beside the Ridge Trail in the preserve in late May.

to New Brunswick's Grand Manan Island. A narrow side trail (suitable for foot traffic only) leads down to the beach, ending in a series of stone steps.

Near the far end of the wheelchair-accessible trail, just before the overlook, the Ridge Trail starts on the left and leads north, traveling through the edge of a wetland over a series of bog bridges. The Ridge Trail then splits into a loop that travels up and over a rocky outcropping and provides breathtaking views of the area. At the far end of the loop, a trail continues north, weaving through a hilly, mossy mixed forest to the rocky shore at Moose Cove. And at the far end of this trail is another loop trail. Round trip, this hike is about 2.3 miles and moderate in difficulty, requiring attention to footing because of the uneven terrain, tree roots, and rocks.

The north parking area also provides access to the Chimney Trail, which forms a 0.7-mile loop and visits the remains of a tall brick chimney by the rocky shore. From the parking area to the chimney, this trail is wide and smooth, surfaced with mowed grass and lined with bushes, making it an excellent place for bird-watching. After the chimney the trail becomes narrower, hillier, and rocky as it travels along the shore, then reenters the forest and loops around to Moose River Road. Along the way is a side trail to a nearby knoll and Bog Brook Road.

Bog Brook Road serves as a connection between the two trail networks in the preserve.

The 1,770-acre preserve is made up of several adjoining parcels that were acquired by the Maine Coast Heritage Trust over time, starting in 2005, with the bulk of the

Spring blossoms add to the beauty of the coastal landscape of the 1,770-acre preserve.

The Ridge Trail in the preserve travels through a mossy forest floor for more than 2 miles, stopping off at a rocky beach on Moose Cove along the way.

land being purchased by the land trust in 2008. The Land for Maine's Future program provided part of the funding for the preserve.

The preserve is adjacent to the 12,234-acre state-owned Cutler Coast Public Reserved Land unit, making it part of the largest contiguous area of conservation land on the Maine coast outside of Acadia National Park, according to the Maine Coast Heritage Trust.

Approximately 88 acres of the preserve are managed for commercial blueberry harvesting, and an estimated 40 percent of the preserve consists of wetland soils. Local wildlife include black bear, bobcat, fisher, and two birds rarely seen in Maine—yellow rail and upland sandpiper.

For more information: Visit www.mcht.org or call the Maine Coast Heritage Trust's East Machias office at (207) 259-5040.

Personal note: With my dog Oreo sitting regally in the front passenger seat of my Subaru, I drove east, windows rolled down, through blueberry barrens and quaint old towns, to the Bold Coast. It was a warm, sunny day in May, and we were headed to Bog Brook Cove Preserve, an outdoor destination about 2 hours east of my home. (Fortunately, Oreo had gotten past the phase where he gets carsick if riding for over an hour.)

Along the way we passed the "Blueberry Dome" of Wild Blueberry Land in Columbia Falls. And in Machias, we drove over the Middle River Reservoir, where the Machias Valley Farmers Market was in full swing, with local flowers, fiddleheads,

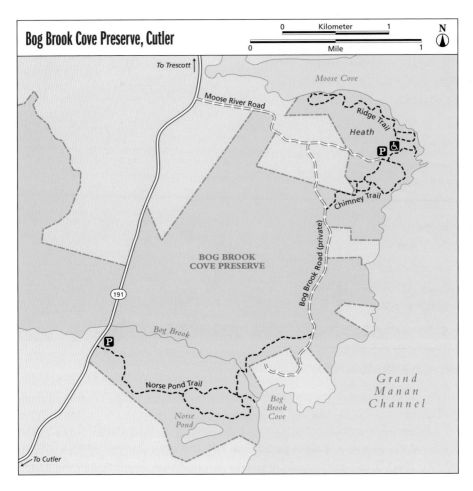

Kilometer

Mile

N

To Trescott

Moose Cove

Moose River Road

Ridge Trail

Heath

P

Chimney Trail

Bog Brook Road (private)

BOG BROOK
COVE PRESERVE

191

Bog Brook

P

Norse Pond Trail

Bog
Brook
Cove

Grand
Manan
Channel

Norse
Pond

To Cutler

and fresh eggs. We then puttered through the coastal village of Cutler, its harbor filled with fishing boats, and on to the neighboring Trescott Township and the north parking area for Bog Brook Cove Preserve, which we found empty.

Our carefree visit at the preserve that day will remain in my memory as a mixture of sun and salty air, smooth cobblestones, serviceberry blossoms, and birdsong. With Oreo at my side, I walked the wheelchair-accessible trail to the beach, where Oreo waded through the frigid water and clambered over seaweed-covered rock formations while I inspected the cobblestones, tumbled round and smooth by the crashing waves of the Atlantic.

We then explored the Ridge Trail and Chimney Trail, traveling over more rugged terrain. Along the way I stopped to photograph a black-and-white warbler and common yellowthroat, two songbirds that appear in the spring and have very self-descriptive names. (The black-and-white warbler is streaked with black and white, and the common yellowthroat has a bright yellow throat and a handsome black mask.) I also spotted several ravens hunting for snacks in the seaweed and raising a

A ridge in the preserve offers great views of the rocky coastline and nearby ocean.

racket with their wild calls. I tried to duplicate their calls as we walked along. Oreo wasn't amused.

By the time we completed both trails, we didn't have time to visit the south parking area to check out the Norse Pond Trail and cobblestone beach of Bog Brook Cove. We'll just have to return another day, which doesn't irk me even the slightest bit. It's always nice to look forward to another adventure.

Hike 30: Viles Arboretum in Augusta

About these trails: In the midst of Maine's capital city, the Viles Arboretum is 224 acres of fields, orchards, gardens, and forests that the public can explore on a 5-mile network of intersecting trails. Most trails are smooth and easy, though there are a few hills and rougher forest trails along the edges of the property.

Difficulty: Easy to moderate, depending on how much of the trail network you choose to tackle. All of the trails add up to about 5 miles in length. Some of the trails are smooth and wide, while some of the forest trails travel over rougher terrain with exposed tree roots.

Dogs: Permitted if on leash at all times. Visitors are expected to pick up after their dogs and dispose of waste properly.

Cost: Free. A green donation container is located near the trailhead kiosk.

Access: The grounds are open to the public from dawn to dusk, year-round. Recreational uses of the land vary from hiking to horseback riding, and in the winter the trail network is a popular place for snowshoeing and cross-country skiing. The arboretum board asks that visitors refrain from climbing on sculptures or picking apples. Bicycles are allowed on trails but must yield to visitors on foot. The Visitor Center is open 8 a.m. to 4 p.m. Monday through Friday year-round, except on holidays.

Wheelchair accessibility: The main trails starting near the Visitor Center—such as the wide, gravel Hosta Trail—were constructed to be accessible by wheelchair, but they may not be ADA compliant. Some of the trails farther into the trail network were not constructed to be accessible by wheelchair.

Hunting: Not permitted.

Restrooms: Located in the Visitor Center.

How to get there: The arboretum is located at 153 Hospital Street in Augusta. If driving south on Interstate 95, take exit 109A; and if driving north on Interstate 95, take exit 109. Both exits lead to Western Avenue, which you follow east for about 1.5 miles to a roundabout. At the roundabout take the second exit to continue on Western Avenue across the Kennebec River. After the bridge, at the next roundabout, take the first exit onto Stone Street (Route 17) and drive 0.5 mile. Continue straight onto Hospital Street, then drive about 0.7 mile and Viles Arboretum will be on your left, marked with a large sign.

GPS coordinates: 44.299664', -69.766849'

The arboretum dates back to 1981, when the Maine Forest Service began its development by planting 120 trees and constructing many fences, bridges, trails, and a boardwalk. The next year, a private nonprofit corporation called the Pine Tree State Arboretum was formed to manage the property, and the following year, a visitor center was built near the parking area.

Over the years, the Viles Arboretum has expanded to house a number of fascinating plant collections, including a rock garden of alpine plants, the state's largest public hosta garden, an heirloom apple tree grove, an American chestnut collection, a large lilac garden, a nut tree collection, and stands of various conifers and deciduous trees.

An heirloom apple orchard is just one of several collections of trees at the arboretum. Visitors are asked not to pick the apples.

A few highlights of the property include "the General Sugar Maple," a giant old sugar maple near the parking area; Viles Pond, home to turtles, waterfowl, and wading birds; and a stand of white pines that as seeds orbited the Earth 93 times, traveling 2.4 million miles, in 1991 on the space shuttle *Atlantis*.

There are also several historical landmarks on the property.

In the early 1800s the property was broken up into several small farms. Then, in 1835, the State Hospital (now Augusta Mental Health Institute) purchased and consolidated the farms into a "hospital farm," which provided crops and livestock, as well as occupational therapy and exercise for hospital patients. Evidence of this history remains on the land. For example, remains of a piggery—once a large three-story barn, heated by burning wood—is identified with an educational sign on one of the arboretum trails.

A detailed map posted on the trailhead kiosk helps visitors find these landmarks, as well as specific gardens and groves of interest.

When the arboretum was established in the early 1980s, it was initially called Pine Tree State Arboretum, but in 2010 it was renamed the Viles Arboretum to honor William Payson Viles (1906–1986) and Elsie Pike Viles (1914–2013), who provided guidance and financial support as the property developed over the years.

In recent years, under the arboretum's "Shifting Gears Initiative," sculptures have been added to the grounds, and interpretive panels for 20 of the botanical collections

A milkweed plant is releasing its seeds in early October at the arboretum.

A plaque tells visitors of the arboretum the significance of a particular white pine grove, which was grown from seeds that orbited the Earth 93 times aboard the space shuttle Atlantis *in 1991.*

have been installed. In addition, the arboretum revamped its plant-labeling process, making it easier for visitors to learn about the plants on display.

For more information: Call (207) 626-7989 or visit www.vilesarboretum.org, where you will find a beautifully illustrated trail map on the "Documents" page, under the "More" tab at the top of the main page.

Personal note: Because of the wide variety of trees growing at the Viles Arboretum, I figured it would be an especially beautiful place to visit in the autumn, when the leaves take on vibrant colors. Autumn is also a time when many fruits, berries, and nuts ripen in Maine, adding more hues and textures to the landscape. So on a fine day in October, I drove south to Augusta to visit the arboretum, which has earned the reputation of being a great place for people to learn about many different plants while getting a little exercise.

On that particular day it still felt like summer, with the sun shining bright and the temperature hovering around 70 degrees. Nevertheless, oak and maple leaves were bleeding from green to reds and oranges.

I spent several hours wandering the arboretum and visited nearly every trail and plant collection. One of my favorite places was the conifer collection, which included a droopy tree called a weeping white pine. I also found the "space shuttle trees" to be fascinating. It was hard to believe that those white pines had orbited the Earth 93 times aboard a space shuttle. I usually think of trees as being such stable, immobile objects—and for good reason, seeing how they're usually rooted to the ground.

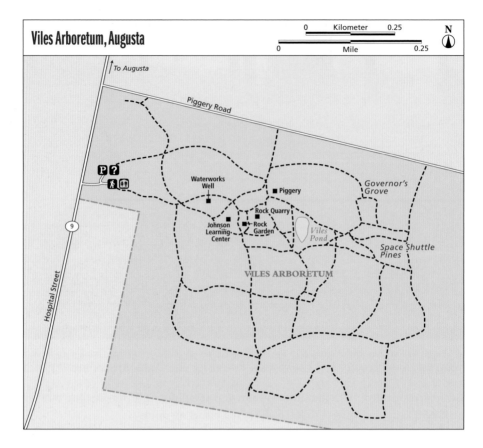

While walking the trail network, I came across several other visitors, including a mother pushing a stroller on a path through the flowering trees collection. In addition to having her newborn baby on the walk with her, she was also accompanied by her mother and 4-year-old son.

Another visitor I remember well is an older man I spoke with as he sat on a bench at the edge of Viles Pond. He told me that he enjoys birding at the arboretum. With all the different habitats on the property, including fields dotted with nesting boxes, it's an especially good place to find a variety of birds.

While I wasn't actively looking for birds, I noticed the shrill call of a pileated woodpecker, as well as a group of friendly chickadees and nuthatches in the shaded hosta garden. I also spotted two eastern painted turtles sunning on a log in the pond. From quite a distance away, they spotted me, then hit the water. Turtles, it seems, have especially good eyesight.

Hike 31 : Rachel Carson National Wildlife Refuge in Wells

About this trail: Named in honor of a famous American environmentalist, the Rachel Carson National Wildlife Refuge was established in 1966 in southern Maine to protect valuable salt marshes and estuaries for migratory birds. Located along 50 miles of coastline in York and Cumberland Counties, the refuge consists of 11 divisions between Kittery and Cape Elizabeth. The trail bearing Carson's name is a great place to start exploring.

Difficulty: Easy. The 1-mile Carson Trail is smooth and wide and forms a loop that begins and ends at the main parking area.

Dogs: Leashed dogs are allowed on the Carson Trail only. All other areas of the refuge are off-limits for dogs. Visitors are expected to pick up after their dogs and dispose of waste properly.

Cost: Free.

Access: Designated visitor use areas (including the Carson Trail) are open to visitors year-round, from sunrise to sunset. However, it's important to note that many areas of the refuge are closed to the public. These areas are marked with boundary signs that read "Area Closed" or "Unauthorized Entry Prohibited." Also, within the refuge, camping, ATVs, bikes, horses, and fires are prohibited.

Wheelchair accessibility: The Carson Trail, as well as the nearby visitor center and restroom, was constructed to be wheelchair accessible.

Hunting: Hunting, fishing, and recreational shellfishing are permitted on the refuge in certain areas and only with specific permits and licenses. The special regulations for these activities are listed at www.fws.gov/refuge/rachel_carson.

Restrooms: Restrooms are located near the Carson Trailhead at the refuge headquarters in Wells and near the Cutts Island Trailhead in the Brave Boat Harbor Division in Kittery.

How to get there: From Interstate 95, take exit 19. At the end of the exit ramp, turn left onto Route 9-Route 109 and drive about 1.5 miles to the traffic light on Route 1. Turn left and drive north on Route 1 for 1.8 miles, then turn right onto Route 9 (Port Road). Drive 0.6 mile and the refuge entrance will be on your right.

GPS coordinates: 43.347437', -70.548563'

Land acquisition for the refuge is ongoing, according to the US Fish and Wildlife Service, but the plan is for the refuge to reach the approximate size of 14,600 acres.

Known as an excellent place for wildlife watching, easy nature walks, and quiet water paddling, the refuge sees between 260,000 and 330,000 visitors from all over the world each year; of those visitors, about 100,000 walk the 1-mile Carson Trail located at the refuge headquarters in Wells.

The Carson Trail forms a loop through a fern-filled forest within the salt marsh surrounding the Branch Brook and Merriland River where they flow together to form the Little River. The easy trail is wide and surfaced with gravel, with wooden observation platforms along the way that offer views of the forest and marsh.

The Merriland River is seen from an outlook on the 1-mile Carson Trail in July.

Before exploring the trail, pick up a brochure at the trailhead kiosk. The brochure includes a detailed trail map and information about the refuge that can be read as a self-guided tour. The brochure text, numbered to match with 11 stations along the trail, touches upon topics including salt marsh restoration, phenology, waterfowl, and shrubland management.

Also along the trail is a memorial plaque for Rachel Carson (1907–1964), an environmentalist and marine biologist who is best known for her influential book *Silent Spring*. Published in 1962, *Silent Spring* was a call to society to take responsibility for other forms of life, focusing on the harmful effects of pesticides, such as DDT, on the natural world. The controversial book pushed the federal government to order a complete review of its pesticide policy and ban DDT.

Born in rural Pennsylvania, Carson had a knack for writing about nature and science in an engaging and poetic way that spoke to the general public. In addition to *Silent Spring*, Carson taught people about nature—and especially the ocean—through newspaper articles, radio programs, and her work as an aquatic biologist and editor-in-chief for the US Fish and Wildlife Service.

Carson died from cancer in 1964 at the age of 57. The refuge, named in honor of her in 1969, is near Carson's summer home on the coast of Maine.

In addition to the Carson Trail, there are two other public trails maintained by the US Fish and Wildlife Service on divisions of the Rachel Carson National Wildlife Refuge: the 1.8-mile Cutts Island Trail in the Brave Boat Harbor Division in Kittery, and the 1.25-mile Timber Point Trail in the Little River Division in Biddeford.

My niece Willamina skips along the easy 1-mile Carson Trail in July at the refuge.

The 1-mile Carson Trail includes several short boardwalks that lead to views of the Merriland River and Branch Brook.

People also can enjoy the refuge by boat. There are three areas within the refuge where nonmotorized canoes and kayaks can launch and land during daylight hours only. These areas are Chauncey Creek, on Seapoint Road in Kittery; Little River, at the end of Granite Point Road in Biddeford; and Spurwink River, at the fish pier on Route 77 in Scarborough.

The US Fish and Wildlife Service asks that refuge visitors follow "Leave No Trace" principles. Carry out all trash (including dog waste) and stay on designated trails to avoid trampling plants and coming into contact with poison ivy and ticks. Disturbing or collecting plants, animals, and artifacts is prohibited.

For more information: Call the refuge office at (207) 646-9226 or visit www.fws .gov/refuge/rachel_carson.

Personal note: In July of 2016, I had a girls weekend in southern Maine with my mom, big sister, and 4½-year-old niece. We stayed at a hotel in Portland, shopped, ate at Sebago Brewing Co., and drove a bit farther south to visit the Rachel Carson National Wildlife Refuge in Wells.

As we began the Carson Trail, my niece Willa snagged the trail brochure from my hands and led the way. Wooden signs marked numbered stations on the trail, so we had her identify the number on each sign, then find it on the map. She got so excited about finding the next number that we had to remind her to slow down, enjoy the views of the marsh, and look at all the different ferns and trees.

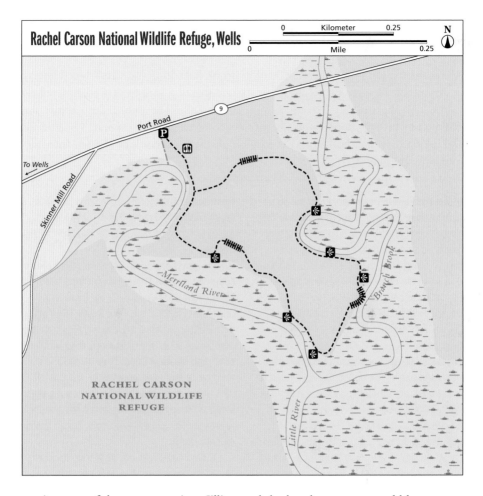

Rachel Carson National Wildlife Refuge, Wells

To Wells

Port Road

Skinner Mill Road

Merriland River

Branch Brook

Little River

RACHEL CARSON
NATIONAL WILDLIFE
REFUGE

At some of the stops, my sister Jillian read the brochure so we could learn more about the salt marsh and the wildlife we might see. Then, mimicking her mother, Willa decided to do the same and "read" to us about butterflies. While standing on a wooden platform in the sun at a beautiful overlook by Branch Brook, we learned from Willa that butterflies like to "fly and swim, eat and drink, and watch people."

The sparrows and tree swallows also slowed Willa down. Once I pointed out the birds, Willa was fascinated. Beside the trail, she patiently crouched near me as I photographed a tree swallow from afar as it fed its nestlings on one of the nesting boxes that were posted throughout the marsh. By the end of the hike, Willa was doing her best to "talk back" to the birds she heard in the forest, tweeting and screeching as she skipped down the smooth trail.

Hike 32: Salmon Brook Lake Trails in Perham

About these trails: The 1,706-acre Salmon Brook Lake Unit is a state-owned reserve in Aroostook County that is home to six rare plants, a variety of wetlands, upland woods, and the shallow, 50-acre Salmon Brook Lake. The public can explore this ecologically diverse property on a beautifully constructed multiuse trail, a boardwalk, and hiking trails that lead to an observation platform overlooking the fen lawn surrounding the lake.

Difficulty: Easy to moderate. From the south parking area, the hike is about 5 miles to the observation platform and back, but much of that is on smooth multiuse trails. From the north parking area, the hike is a little less than 3 miles to the observation platform and back, or 4 miles to the group shelter and back.

Dogs: Permitted if kept under control at all times. Carry out all pet waste.

Cost: Free.

Access: Trails are open year-round. In the winter the parking lot on Tangle Ridge Road is not plowed, but the parking lot at the Perham Town Office is plowed.

Wheelchair accessibility: The trail leading from the multiuse Bangor and Aroostook Trail to the group shelter and boat launch on Salmon Brook was constructed to be wheelchair accessible, though it may not meet ADA standards. The trail from there to the observation platform and the Tangle Ridge Road trailhead is not wheelchair accessible; it's narrow and includes exposed tree roots, rocks, and narrow bog bridges. The outhouse is not wheelchair accessible.

Hunting: Permitted in accordance with state laws, but the discharge of any weapon is prohibited from or within 300 feet of any picnic area, camping area or campsite, parking area, building, shelter, boat launch site, posted trail, or other developed area.

Restrooms: An outhouse is located near the group shelter by Salmon Brook, where the multiuse trail ends and the narrower hiking trail begins.

How to get there: To hike the trails from the south, park at the Perham Town Office off High Meadow Road in Perham. To get there from downtown Presque Isle, take Route 164 (Washburn Road) and drive 10.4 miles, then turn left onto Route 228. Drive 7.4 miles, then turn left onto High Meadow Road. Drive 1 mile and the town office and town park will be on your left. Park there, then start the hike by crossing High Meadow Road and walking east a few hundred feet to the Bangor and Aroostook Trail (a gravel multiuse trail).

You can also hike the trails from the north. This is a shorter hike that does not include any walking along the multiuse Bangor and Aroostook Trail. To get to the north parking lot from the Perham Town Office, drive 1.2 mile west on High Meadow Road, then turn right onto Tangle Ridge Road. Drive 3.2 miles and the gravel parking area will be on your right. The trail starts by the kiosk in the parking lot, which is across the road from a large farmhouse.

GPS coordinates: South parking lot 46.878142', -68.241125'; North parking lot 46.916606', -68.249272'

I walk along a boardwalk of the Salmon Brook Lake Trail with my dog, Oreo.

The Salmon Brook Lake Unit is dominated by what's known as an unpatterned fen ecosystem, and within this ecosystem are several natural communities. For example, surrounding the lake is a 65-acre sedge-leatherleaf fen lawn, home to leatherleaf, sweet gale, and slender sedge. North of the lake is a shrubby cinquefoil-sedge circumneutral fen surrounded by spruce and cedar swamps. And south of the lake is a spruce-larch wooded bog.

Rare plants in the property include small, round-leaved orchis, lapland buttercup, showy lady's slipper, swamp fly-honeysuckle, marsh valerian, and pygmy water-lily, according to the Maine Natural Areas Program.

The unit is connected to the multiuse Bangor and Aroostook Trail, which travels along the old railroad bed of the Bangor and Aroostook Railway and is 61 miles long. This trail is open to ATVs, horseback riders, bicyclists, and walkers. In the winter it is open to cross-country skiers, snowshoers, dog sleds, and snowmobilers.

The Salmon Brook Lake Unit can be accessed from two trailheads.

The south trailhead is at the Perham Town Office. From there you have to walk 1.28 miles along the Bangor and Aroostook Trail to the Calvin Wardwell Salmon Brook Lake Trail, which leads into the Salmon Brook Lake Unit and is also open to ATVs. The 0.2-mile trail, dedicated in 2008, includes a wide wooden boardwalk that leads through a beautiful cedar swamp. The trail ends at a group shelter, picnic table, and outhouse near Salmon Brook.

At the group shelter you'll find the start of a narrow hiking trail that travels through a mixed forest for 0.5 mile to a boardwalk and large observation platform in

A boardwalk on the Salmon Brook Lake Trail offers an open view of Salmon Brook Lake and the surrounding wetlands.

the fen surrounding Salmon Brook Lake, which reaches only 5 feet at its deepest and has an average depth of around 2 feet. This is a great place for wildlife watching and picnicking. Wooden benches are located along the edges of the platform.

From the observation platform, the hiking trail continues north through the forest for another 0.9 mile, where it reaches a trail intersection. If you turn left, you'll soon reach the Bangor and Aroostook Trail, where you can turn left and walk a little over 2 miles back to the trailhead at the Perham Town Office. Or you can turn right at the trail intersection and hike 0.5 mile to the north parking lot on Tangle Ridge Road.

The north parking area and trailhead were created for people who would prefer not to walk along the multiuse Bangor and Aroostook Trail in order to visit Salmon Brook Pond.

The Maine Bureau of Parks and Lands' Off-Road Vehicle Division, BPL's Northern Region Lands Office, and the town of Perham all partner to manage the Salmon Brook Pond trails.

For more information: Call BPL's Northern Region Lands Office at (207) 435-7963, ext. 209, or send an e-mail to vern.labbe@maine.gov.

Personal note: Packed into an old SUV, my family and I—along with our dog Oreo—made the long drive up to Aroostook County in early August to camp in a rustic cabin on the shore of Echo Lake in Presque Isle. With a cargo carrier strapped to the top of the vehicle and a giant cooler full of food fastened to the back hitch, we were ready for a weekend of campfires, hiking, swimming, and fishing.

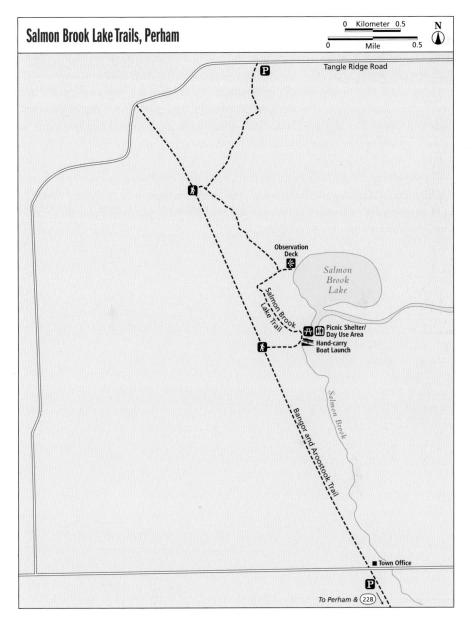

Salmon Brook Lake Trails, Perham

0   Kilometer   0.5

0   Mile   0.5

N

Tangle Ridge Road

P

Observation Deck

Salmon Brook Lake

Salmon Brook Lake Trail

Picnic Shelter/ Day Use Area

Hand-carry Boat Launch

Salmon Brook

Bangor and Aroostook Trail

Town Office

P

To Perham & 228

On the itinerary was a hike on the Salmon Brook Lake trails, which were located just about 35 minutes northwest of our camping area. Having read about the trails online, I thought they'd be the perfect day hike for our group, which included my husband, my mother-in-law, and her significant other. Oreo is game for any type of hike, long or short, so I knew I could please him. But I didn't want to select anything too long or difficult for the rest of the group.

We hiked from the south parking area at the Perham Town Office, which may have been a poor decision on my part because the hike ended up being a bit longer than we anticipated. If we'd hiked from the north, it would have been shorter. Nevertheless, we had a great time, and the trails exceeded our expectations.

Seemingly out in the middle of nowhere, the trails were well constructed and maintained, and the wooden bridges, boardwalks, and platforms were impressively built and in good condition. Then there were the many beautiful habitats the trails visited, including the sedge-leatherleaf fen lawn where the observation deck was located.

In the woods we had fun pointing out a variety of bright mushrooms, berries, and wildflowers. And along the Bangor and Aroostook multiuse trail, we found some old railway ties, and I managed to photograph a few different species of butterflies as they fluttered from wildflower to wildflower.

Hike 33: Aroostook National Wildlife Refuge, East Loring Division, in Limestone

About these trails: Comprising 7,750 acres in northern Maine, the Aroostook National Wildlife Refuge includes part of the former Loring Air Force Base, a key military facility throughout the Cold War. From 1950 to 1994 the Strategic Air Command was stationed at the base, flying long-range bombers capable of delivering nuclear weapons. And in the northeast corner of the site, the Caribou Air Force Station served as a top-secret, self-contained nuclear weapons storage base. These days, the East Loring Division of the refuge is home to 6.4 miles of trails and a 2-mile road that can also be walked or biked.

Difficulty: Easy to moderate. The easiest trail on the property is the 1.2-mile Don Lima Trail, which is wide and surfaced with mowed grass in the fields and gravel in the forest.

Dogs: Permitted if on a leash no longer than 10 feet at all times. Carry out all pet waste.

Cost: Free.

Access: The refuge trails are open to the public seven days a week, from 30 minutes before sunrise to 30 minutes after sunset. Office staff fluctuates throughout the year. The Friends of Aroostook National Wildlife Refuge Gift Store (located in the office building) is open 1 to 4 p.m. Tuesday and Wednesday, and 11 a.m. to 3 p.m. Saturday and Sunday. The trails are for foot traffic only. Bike riding is permitted only on the Auto Tour Route.

Wheelchair accessibility: The 1.2-mile Don Lima Trail (also known as the Nature Trail) was constructed to be wheelchair accessible but may not meet ADA standards, mainly because some areas of the trail may be too soft during certain times of year. The other trails in the East Loring Division were not constructed to be wheelchair accessible.

Hunting: Not permitted.

Restrooms: The only public restrooms on the refuge are located in the building where the offices, visitor center, and nature store are located. This building is open 1 to 4 p.m. Tuesday and Wednesday, and 11 a.m. to 3 p.m. Saturday and Sunday, and may be open at other times, depending on staffing.

How to get there: The address of the refuge office and visitor center is 97 Refuge Road in Limestone. To get there from Route 1 in the nearby town of Caribou, take Route 89 (Access Highway) east 7.3 miles and turn left onto Commerce Center Road. Drive 1.1 miles, then veer right on a bend to stay on Commerce Center Road. Drive 0.2 mile and turn right onto Refuge Road. Drive 0.2 mile and turn right onto the driveway leading to the refuge visitor center and headquarters. As of fall 2016, that is the only parking area for the East Loring Division trails, though there are plans for a second parking lot to open by Beaver Pond Trail in the near future. This future parking area is already shown on the refuge trail map.

GPS coordinates: 46.934575', -67.870120'

Aroostook National Wildlife Refuge was established in 1998, when land was transferred from the US Air Force to the US Fish and Wildlife Service, which immediately took measures to welcome a variety of wildlife back to the site. Since then, military buildings have been demolished on the property, and areas with contaminated soils have been cleaned up.

Today, old weapons bunkers and other traces of the base remain on the property, which is quickly transitioning back into the hands of Mother Nature.

The refuge now features more than 13 miles of public hiking trails split between two separate parcels of land. The East Loring Division of the refuge includes 8.4 miles of hiking trails/walkable road, while the Greenlaw Brook Division features 5.1 miles of trails.

For this entry I'll focus on the East Loring Division, where the refuge office, visitor center, and nature store are located, as well as an easy interpretive nature trail and two photo blinds for wildlife watchers.

The most popular trail on the East Loring Division, the 1.2-mile Don Lima Trail, forms a loop that begins and ends at the refuge office and visitor center. Throughout the trail are detailed interpretive displays with text and illustrations of local wildlife and important habitats seen along the way, such as vernal pools and other types of wetlands. Also along the Don Lima Trail are signs identifying a variety of trees, including tamarack, balsam fir, white birch, and quaking aspen.

A sign marks the 1.2-mile Don Lima Trail behind the visitor center at the East Loring division of the refuge.

A beaver gnaws the bark off a stick while swimming near its lodge in the refuge.

Another highlight of the Don Lima Trail is a photo blind located by a beaver lodge and wetlands. This small green building is the perfect spot for visitors to watch for wildlife (and escape some of the bugs). Animals commonly spotted at the refuge include chickadee, spruce and ruffed grouses, black-backed woodpecker, blackburnian and bay breasted warblers, hermit thrush, American woodcock, northern goshawk, bald eagle, moose, white-tailed deer, snowshoe hare, beaver, lynx, river otter, mink, ermine, and coyote, according to the US Fish and Wildlife Service.

If you're looking for a longer hike, the Don Lima Trail leads to the 3.5-mile East Loring Trail, which is wide and surfaced with mowed grass. This trail strikes north through the refuge to the 1-mile Durepo Loop Trail and 0.7-mile Beaver Pond Trail. The East Loring Trail ends with a small loop east of East Loring Lake.

The Aroostook National Wildlife Refuge is a part of the Northern Maine National Wildlife Refuge Complex, which also includes Moosehorn National Wildlife Refuge, which is just north of Machias, and Sunkhaze National Wildlife Refuge, which is just north of Bangor. All three refuges feature public trails that are great for families.

For more information: Call the refuge offices in Limestone at (207) 328-4634, or call the administrative offices for the Northern Maine Refuge Complex at (207) 454-1700, or visit www.fws.gov/refuge/Aroostook, where detailed trail maps are available.

Personal note: I first visited Aroostook National Wildlife Refuge in May of 2013 to learn about an odd experiment scientists were conducting to learn more about white-nose syndrome, a disease that has been killing off certain species of bats for

A duck nesting box is located near a beaver lodge and pond near the Don Lima Trail in the refuge.

several years now. Biologists from throughout the northeast were working with the refuge to create artificial hibernacula (bat caves) in old weapons bunkers on the property. Their hope was that these sterilized bunkers would help the bats survive.

The experiment wasn't wildly successful, but it did help biologists learn more about white-nose syndrome and the use of artificial hibernacula.

More than three years later, I returned to refuge on an entirely different mission—to walk its Don Lima Trail and learn more about the recreational opportunities on the property.

The refuge is a few hours from where I live in the Bangor area, so I made a weekend trip of it with my husband Derek; our dog Oreo; Derek's mom, Geneva; and Geneva's partner, John. We set up camp in Presque Isle on Friday evening, not far from Aroostook State Park, then spent the weekend exploring the area.

By the time we drove up to Limestone to visit the refuge, it was Sunday, and we were tired from two late nights playing a dice game called Tenzi by lantern light, swimming in Echo Lake, eating copious amounts of food, enjoying homemade mojitos, and hiking area trails.

The easy Don Lima Trail was the perfect walk for weary travelers. We moved slowly, which gave us the chance to notice the small things—such as moose tracks in the mud, a yellow crab spider perched on a black-eyed Susan, and little pink bell-shaped flowers I'd never seen before. (Back at home, I did some searching on the Internet, and I believe they were a European wildflower called bladder campion, a

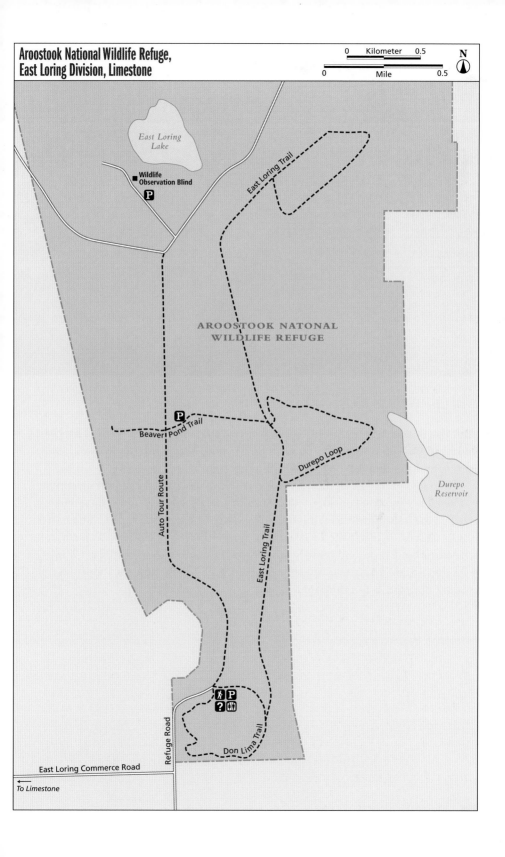

Aroostook National Wildlife Refuge, East Loring Division, Limestone

0　Kilometer　0.5

0　Mile　0.5

N

East Loring Lake

Wildlife Observation Blind

East Loring Trail

AROOSTOOK NATONAL WILDLIFE REFUGE

Beaver Pond Trail

Auto Tour Route

Durepo Loop

Durepo Reservoir

East Loring Trail

Don Lima Trail

Refuge Road

East Loring Commerce Road

To Limestone

My husband Derek and our dog Oreo lead the way while walking the 1.2-mile Don Lima Trail in the refuge with other family members.

plant that is now widespread in North America and considered a weed. This plant flowers in mid-June, so by the time we came across it up north, the blossoms were starting to dry into what looked like tiny paper lanterns.)

The most exciting part of our hike was when we spotted a beaver swimming in a pond not far from a beaver lodge. Standing on a grassy hill above the pond, we watched the beaver for several minutes (me photographing it with glee). The beaver was so close to us—and the forest was so quiet—that we could hear its teeth as it scraped bark off sticks and munched on leaves. I could also watch its flat tail move from side to side, acting as a rudder as it swam. And several times, it slapped its tail, creating a big splash as it dove underwater.

Hike 34: Coastal Maine Botanical Gardens in Boothbay

About these trails: A place so beautiful it's almost overwhelming, the Coastal Maine Botanical Gardens opened in 2007 after more than 15 years of planning, building, and planting. Located in the midcoast town of Boothbay, this outdoor destination comprises 270 acres of tidal shoreland and features several miles of trails that wind through a wide variety of themed gardens and coastal woods.

Difficulty: Easy to moderate, depending on the trails you choose to explore. Several paths in the Central Gardens are wide, smooth, and built to be wheelchair accessible. Trails outside the Central Gardens vary in difficulty; some are wide and surfaced with compacted gravel, while others are more challenging, traveling over unimproved forest floor with rocks and roots.

Dogs: Dogs are not permitted in the gardens (unless they are service animals), but they are permitted in the parking areas and on the adjacent dog trail if on leash at all times. There is a water spigot and water dish for pets in the picnic area beside the southernmost parking lot. Visitors are expected to pick up after their dogs; the gardens provide plastic bags for picking up dog waste, as well as trash bags where you can dispose of the waste.

Hunting: Not permitted.

Cost: Admission is $16 for adults, $14 for seniors (65+), and $8 for children 3–17 years old; children younger than 3 years old are free. Garden members also receive free admission, and there are special rates for groups, schools, and camps.

Access: The gardens are open to the public 9 a.m. to 5 p.m. April 15 through October 31, with hours extended to 6 p.m. in July and August. Bicycles and active sports such as kite flying and Frisbee are not permitted in the gardens. Barbecuing and smoking are also prohibited.

Wheelchair accessibility: The Visitor Center and Central Gardens are ADA compliant, and there are benches placed throughout the grounds for visitors to rest. In addition, the gardens provide wheelchairs on loan at no charge on a first-come, first-served basis; and scooters are available to rent for $16 on a first-come, first-served basis for use in the Central Gardens.

Restrooms: Located in the Visitor Center.

How to get there: The entrance to the gardens is on Barters Island Road in Boothbay. For GPS users the physical address is 132 Botanical Gardens Drive. To get there from the Boothbay monument on Route 27, across from the town common and gazebo, turn onto Corey Lane and drive 0.4 mile, then turn right onto Barters Island Road. Drive 1 mile, and the entrance to the gardens will be on your left, Botanical Gardens Drive.

GPS coordinates: 43.876713, -69.657189

Key features of the gardens include the Vayo Meditation Garden; the Burpee Kitchen Garden; multiple scenic ponds filled with lily pads and frogs; a rose and perennial garden with a large rose arbor; the Lerner Garden of the Five Senses; a woodland garden; a garden of rare and extraordinary plants; a rhododendron garden; the Bosarge

A greenhouse and learning garden designed to engage children is one of the many features of the Coastal Maine Botanical Gardens.

Family Education Center; and the Great Lawn, where events often take place behind the Visitor Center.

In addition, many areas in the gardens were constructed especially for children, including the whimsical Bibby and Harold Alfond Children's Garden, home to a greenhouse, coloring cottage, story barn, maze lawn, scenic blueberry pond, and whale stone sculptures that spout water, for those who'd like to cool off. Also, tucked in the woods nearby is a giant treehouse, a structure called the Bear Cave, and a fairy house garden, where visitors can build their own fairy houses with natural materials.

Visitors should start their exploration of the gardens at the Visitor Center, where you can collect a trail map and pay admission at an information desk. Once you pay admission, you'll be given a sticker to display on your clothing during your visit.

Also in the Visitor Center is a well-stocked gift store and the Kitchen Garden Cafe, open 11 a.m. to 3 p.m. daily.

While many of the paths in the Central Gardens were constructed to be accessible by wheelchair, the trails outside the Central Gardens become more challenging as the terrain includes more hills and trails enter the forest. Some trails are wide and surfaced with compacted gravel, while other trails are more traditional hiking trails over unimproved forest floor. These woodland trails stretch for several miles, visiting a waterfall and tracing the shore of Huckleberry Cove and Back River, where a boat landing is located with kayaks for rent.

Along the trails, and throughout the gardens, are educational displays on various topics pertaining to the gardens, as well as the natural landscape. There are also permanent and temporary sculptures scattered throughout the gardens by a wide variety of artists, and rotating art exhibits in the Visitor Center, Kitchen Garden Cafe, and Education Center.

The gardens provide several special tours and services, all of which can be learned about at the Visitor Center. For example, the gardens offer kayak tours led by a registered guide; tours on the *Beagle*, the first fully electric Coast Guard–certified vessel in Maine; and one-hour tours of the gardens by quiet electric carts, led by trained docents. Call ahead at least one week prior to your visit to make reservations.

In the gardens visitors are asked to walk only on the paths or lawns and to leave plants and wildlife undisturbed. Children must be supervised at all times. Also, keep in mind that the gates are locked at closing. Exit before then.

For more information: Call (207) 633-8000 or visit www.mainegardens.org.

Personal note: The Coastal Maine Botanical Gardens is a special place to me and my husband Derek, because it's the location of one of our first dates back in 2009. At the time, the gardens had been open for only two years, and they were still expanding.

Across the man-made Blueberry Pond, visitors to the gardens explore the Bibby and Harold Alfond Children's Garden.

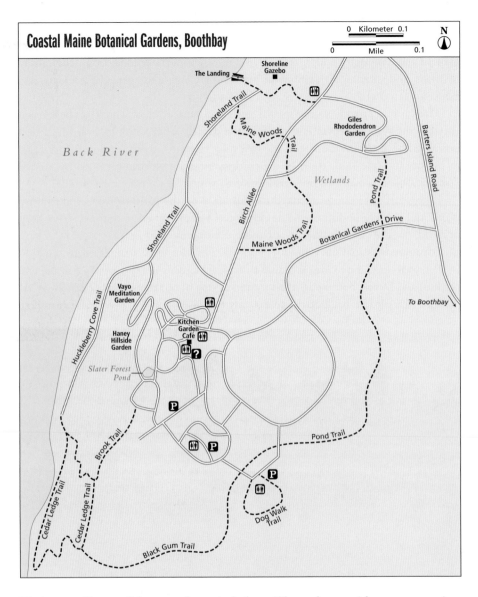

Coastal Maine Botanical Gardens, Boothbay

The Landing

Shoreline Gazebo

Back River

Maine Woods Trail

Shoreland Trail

Giles Rhododendron Garden

Barters Island Road

Wetlands

Pond Trail

Birch Allée

Maine Woods Trail

Botanical Gardens Drive

Shoreland Trail

To Boothbay

Huckleberry Cove Trail

Vayo Meditation Garden

Kitchen Garden Cafe

Haney Hillside Garden

Slater Forest Pond

P

Brook Trail

P

Pond Trail

P

Cedar Ledge Trail

Cedar Ledge Trail

Dog Walk Trail

Black Gum Trail

Yet it was still one of the most fantastical places I'd ever been, with a greater variety of plants than I'd ever seen, metal animal sculptures lurking on perfectly manicured lawns, and children building fairy houses in the woods.

The next year, in August 2010, I returned to the gardens to write a story about the Maine Fairy House Festival, which was so popular that it is now a weekly event in July and August called "Fairy Fridays," with a full schedule of fairy activities, including puppet shows, stories and crafts, fairy yoga, and music and dancing with the Great Bubble Machine. Picture hundreds of children wearing sparkly wings, dancing amidst flower beds and through the woods. It's quite a magical event.

A monarch caterpillar clings to a milkweed plant in the gardens in mid August.

My third (and Derek's second) visit to the gardens came on Sunday, August 14, 2016. It was a sunny, hot day, and we were both tired after an eventful weekend in Portland for my 10th high school reunion. Yet I managed to convince Derek that we'd be remiss to not stop by the gardens on the way home for a stroll through the flowers.

Walking from the parking lot to the Visitor Center to pay admission, I kept pausing to photograph different flowers with my macro lens, saying things like, "I've never seen this type before!" and "Oh, look at the color of that one!" Looking back on the whole visit, I feel slightly guilty. While I was in photographer's heaven, Derek was probably not having quite as much fun on such a hot, sunny day. I kept looking up from my camera to see him waiting patiently in the nearest patch of shade.

The absolute best part of our visit, for me, was spotting a monarch butterfly and getting the opportunity to photograph it as it drew nectar from a bundle of purple flowers. Monarchs used to be very common in Maine, but in recent years their numbers have plummeted due to several factors, including the destruction of their winter habitat in Mexico and the depletion of milkweed, their primary food source, throughout North America. So to see one of these large, stunning butterflies—with its bright orange wings veined in black, and its black body dotted with white—was such a treat.

Derek and I wandered the gardens for a few hours, taking the time to duck into the forest on the Brook Trail, which we followed to Huckleberry Cove. On a bench by the cove, we enjoyed the breeze coming off the water. Then we hiked along the

An educational display on the Shoreland Trail of the gardens offers information about native mosses and lichens.

shore and uphill to the meditation garden, where I couldn't help but dip my hands in water held by a giant stone bowl made by sculptor David Holmes.

Before leaving the gardens, I stopped into the gift store and was pleasantly surprised to see so many interesting nature- and garden-themed items. Exercising restraint, I selected one thing to buy: a Coastal Maine Botanical Gardens T-shirt with a luna moth on the chest.

Hike 35: Sandy Stream Pond and Roaring Brook Nature Trails in Baxter State Park

About these trails: Located in the heart of Maine, Baxter State Park is a beautiful, mountainous stretch of wilderness that includes the state's tallest and most sacred mountain, which was named Katahdin long ago by the Abenaki people. The word means "greatest mountain." Rising 5,268 feet above sea level, Katahdin's rocky ridges and bare peaks attract the majority of visitors that drive into Baxter State Park, but there's much more within the park to explore, including the two short trails described here.

Difficulty: Easy to moderate. The trails include a long series of narrow bog bridges. Watch out for rocks and exposed tree roots. Change in elevation is minimal. The hike to Sandy Stream Pond and back is 0.8 mile, and the nearby Roaring Brook Nature Trail—out, around a loop, and back—is also 0.8 mile. The Roaring Brook Nature Trail is more difficult than the Sandy Stream Pond Trail. It is narrower and includes more exposed tree roots and narrow bog bridges.

Dogs: Not permitted anywhere in the park.

Cost: Day-use pass for vehicles is free for Maine residents (with a Maine driver's license and registration) and $14 for nonresidents. Park cabins, bunkhouses, lean-tos, campsites, and tent sites may be reserved for different fees.

Access: The trails are for foot traffic only. The maximum size of hiking groups is limited to 12 persons. Affiliated groups on the same trail separated by less than one mile will be considered one group. All people entering the park by road or trail must register their entrance at the first opportunity at a staffed gatehouse or self-registration station.

During the summer and fall, Roaring Brook Campground day parking fills up quickly, especially on weekends. However, you may be able to reserve a day parking spot ahead of time by calling (207) 723-5140. Camping is permitted by reservation only and only in authorized campgrounds and campsites May 15 through October 15, and December 1 through March 31.

The gates to Baxter State Park close for the winter, barring vehicles from the park roads. During this time visitors must enter the park on foot and travel by ski, snowshoe, or snowmobile. Snowmobiles are only allowed on the Park Tote Road.

Wheelchair accessibility: The trails are not constructed to be wheelchair accessible. They feature many barriers, including exposed tree roots, rocks, and narrow bog bridges.

Hunting: Not permitted in the area of these specific trails.

Restrooms: Several outhouses are located near the Roaring Brook parking lot.

How to get there: Travel on Interstate 95 to exit 244. Turn west on Route 157 and travel through Medway, East Millinocket, and Millinocket. Bear right at the three-way intersection after the second traffic light in downtown Millinocket. Bear left at the next Y intersection, staying on the main road. Drive approximately 14 miles to Togue Pond Gatehouse, the south entrance of Baxter State Park. After registering at the gatehouse, veer right at the Y intersection and drive about 8 miles to Roaring Brook Campground, which is located at the very end of the gravel dead-end road.

GPS coordinates: 45.919692', -68.857365'

Today, Baxter State Park comprises more than 200,000 acres, including more than 40 peaks and ridges in addition to Katahdin. The park's trail system is made up of more than 215 miles of trails, and the park also operates eight roadside campgrounds, two backcountry campgrounds, and numerous individual backcountry sites for backpackers.

All of the trails that scale the famous Katahdin are considered very strenuous and are only appropriate for experienced hikers. Furthermore, no children under the age of six years are allowed above timberline—where the trees disappear at high elevations. Therefore, many of the summits of the park are inaccessible to young children. However, there are many easy-to-moderate trails in the park that lead to views of the mountains, bubbling brooks, waterfalls, and scenic ponds.

Two of these easy, family friendly trails in Baxter State Park are the Sandy Stream Pond Trail and the Roaring Brook Nature Trail, both of which are accessed from the Roaring Brook parking lot. If planning to hike these trails during the summer, it would be best to go on a weekday, early in the morning. The Roaring Brook Campground parking lot usually fills up early in the day because it is also the parking lot for the popular Chimney Pond Trail up Katahdin. To ensure you'll be successful at

A sign beside Sandy Stream Pond Trail reminds hikers to stay on the bog bridges and marked trails.

Katahdin, Maine's tallest mountain, is seen across Sandy Stream Pond in August.

getting a parking space at this parking lot, you can call Baxter State Park headquarters ahead of time to reserve a day-use parking space. Also, Togue Pond Gatehouse issues "Moose Passes," good for three hours per pass, on a first-come, first-served basis.

After registering for your hike—Sandy Stream Pond or Roaring Brook Nature Trail or both—at the Roaring Brook Campground ranger station, you'll start your hike on the wide, rocky trail that runs through the campground, then begin on Chimney Pond Trail. Soon, you'll reach an intersection marked with detailed signs. There, turn right onto Russell Pond Trail, crossing a wide wooden bridge over Roaring Brook.

The Roaring Brook Nature Trail is on your right after the bridge. Starting as a fairly wide trail, crisscrossed with exposed tree roots, the Roaring Brook Nature Trail travels along the edge of beautiful Roaring Brook, its clear water tumbling over granite boulders and pebbles to the right of the path. You'll then cross several wooden footbridges, some of them quite narrow, as the trail moves away from the brook. Expect to navigate over tangles of big tree roots.

About 0.2 mile in, the trail splits into a loop that visits wetlands where you'll likely spy some wildlife. Also, keep your eye out for a variety of mushrooms and interesting woodland plants. Expect rough terrain but no significant change in elevation. Just follow the loop all the way around, then retrace your steps to the parking lot.

The other option—the Sandy Stream Pond Trail—is a bit easier to navigate and a favorite among wildlife enthusiasts because it leads to one place in the park where visitors frequently find moose: Sandy Stream Pond. To find the trail, follow the same

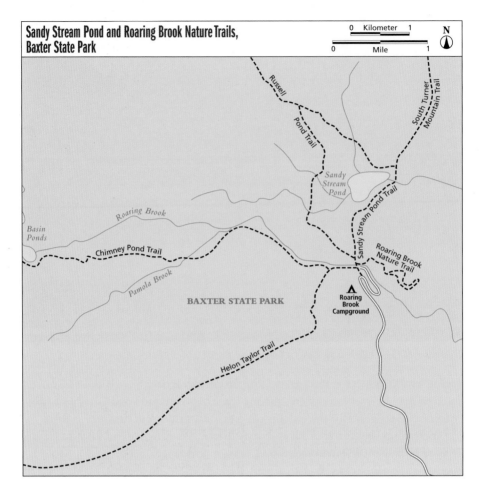

Russell

Pond Trail

Sandy
Stream
Pond

Sandy Stream Pond Trail

South Turner
Mountain Trail

Roaring Brook

Basin
Ponds

Roaring Brook
Nature Trail

Chimney Pond Trail

Pamola Brook

BAXTER STATE PARK

Roaring
Brook
Campground

Helon Taylor Trail

directions, but instead of turning onto the Roaring Brook Nature Trail, continue straight on the Russell Pond Trail and soon you'll reach an intersection where you can veer right onto Sandy Stream Pond Trail.

This trail is fairly smooth and wide, with some rocks and exposed tree roots, and near the pond, it includes a long series of sturdy bog bridges. On this trail it's about 0.4 mile to Sandy Stream Pond.

At the pond two side trails branch off the main trail and lead to the edge of the pond. The first of these trails loops back to the main trail, and the second leads to a large granite boulder that is a great place for a group of people to sit and watch for wildlife or simply take in the stunning view of the pond and Katahdin rising beyond. Often, you'll find a nature photographer with a tripod set up near the pond, waiting for a moose to emerge.

While moose are often seen wading in the pond, eating aquatic plants, you can't count on that always being the case. Don't be discouraged if you don't see a moose. There are plenty of other things to see at the pond, including an amazing view of

A cedar waxwing perches on a branch beside Sandy Stream Pond.

Katahdin and a variety of birds. Waterfowl frequent the pond, and osprey fish its waters.

Also, it's important to remember to give wildlife their space. While moose and deer are generally gentle creatures, they have been known to act unpredictably and even charge at visitors, probably due to habituation. Out of respect, observe wildlife at a distance. This is a great hike for you to bring binoculars or a camera with a magnifying lens. Also, out of respect for wildlife and other observers, it's important to talk quietly (or not at all) while at the edge of the pond.

Sandy Stream Pond Trail continues past the pond to South Turner Mountain, which rises 3,122 feet above sea level and is a popular hike in the park. Therefore, this trail may seem a bit crowded in comparison to the Roaring Brook Nature Trail.

Baxter State Park was a gift to the Maine people by Percival P. Baxter, governor of Maine from 1921 to 1924. An avid outdoorsman, Baxter enjoyed fishing and vacationing in the Maine woods throughout his childhood, and his love of the wilderness led him to create the park during the period from 1930 to 1962, starting with a 6,000-acre parcel that included Katahdin. Over the years, parcel by parcel, Baxter donated this land to the state of Maine with the condition that it be kept forever wild.

Since then, additional purchases and land gifts have expanded the park's total size to 209,644 acres. About 75 percent of the park is managed as a wildlife sanctuary, and about 25 of percent of the park is open to hunting and trapping with the exception of moose hunting, which is prohibited in the park.

For more information: Visit www.baxterstateparkauthority.com or call the park at (207) 723-5140.

Personal note: Nearly two decades ago, my aunt and uncle brought their two young children to camp and hike in Baxter State Park. What began with a small group grew over the years to include more family and friends, including my mom and I, and later, my husband, his mom, and her significant other.

Today, the group consists of multiple families—some related by blood, and others simply connected by their love of the Maine outdoors. And the annual outing has become so popular that we now plan it for two weekends each summer, not just one. That way, if you can't attend one date, perhaps you can attend the other.

Sometimes the group is as small as 15 people, and sometimes it's as big as 35. It all depends on the campground space available and people's schedules. Over the past 10 years at least, I've made it a point to always attend at least one of the trips every year. It's an event I look forward to for several reasons: the good company and food, the campfires and relaxation, the hiking and swimming. For me, Baxter State Park is not only a place to enjoy beautiful mountains, it's a place to unwind with family and old friends, and it's a place to make new friends and lasting memories.

Over the years, I've gotten to know the park quite well. While I often hike trails on Katahdin, I've also explored quite a few of the other trails in the park, including Roaring Brook Nature Trail and Sandy Stream Pond Trail. In fact, I've walked to Sandy Stream Pond many times with the hope of seeing moose and other wildlife. It's a nice, short hike that almost everyone who attends the group camping trip can enjoy.

Sometimes we see moose at the pond, and sometimes we don't. If I've learned one thing about Maine wildlife, it's that, while animals have patterns of behavior, you can never count on them being at a specific location at an exact time. One day I was lucky enough to see two moose wading in Sandy Stream Pond, eating vegetation, while on another day, I visited the pond three times and never saw a moose. Nevertheless, there was plenty of other wildlife to watch at the pond that day. There were cedar waxwings flitting about the evergreens bordering the pond, their smooth feathers the color of orange and yellow sherbet.

Also that day at the pond, I spotted a yellow-rumped warbler in the bushes, an osprey wheeling overhead, and two species of ducks—common mergansers and common goldeneyes—swimming far offshore. The goldeneyes were juveniles, their brown eyes yet to turn gold. And coiled on a rock at the edge of the pond, a large garter snake basked in the sun.

Hike Index

About the Author

Aislinn Sarnacki is a reporter for the *Bangor Daily News* (BDN), a major news outlet in Maine, writing chiefly for the Outdoors section. Her beat for the news includes outdoor recreation, wildlife, and conservation. She also writes a weekly column about hiking trails, which appear in print and on her BDN blog, "Act Out with Aislinn" with photos and videos. To date, she estimates that she has explored at least 250 hiking trails and trail networks throughout the state.

A lifelong Maine resident, Aislinn grew up in Winterport, a small town located on the Penobscot River. While earning a bachelor's degree in journalism from the University of Maine in Orono, she was awarded "Highest Honors" from the University of Maine Honors College for her creative thesis, in which she explored the health benefits of hiking.

In 2012, Aislinn was the recipient of the Bob Drake Young Writer's Award, which is presented each year to a journalist with less than two years' experience whose work demonstrates ability and great potential. More recently, the Maine Press Association named her the top features and lifestyle blogger in Maine for 2014 and 2016.

Aislinn and her husband Derek, along with their dog Oreo and two cats Bo and Arrow, live on a wooded hill overlooking a lake in the Bangor area.

Visit her BDN blog at actoutwithaislinn.bangordailynews.com.

BRIAN FEULNER